TWIN FLAMES

——— ✦ ———

The Journey

By:

POONAM KHAN

Contents

Poonam Khan is a passionate writer and spiritual seeker dedicated to exploring the depths of human connection, self-discovery, and the mysteries of the soul. With a deep interest in the esoteric and metaphysical, Poonam delves into the complexities of twin flame relationships, divine timing, and the journey toward self-love and inner peace. Through a blend of personal experience and spiritual insight, she offers a unique perspective on the transformative power of love and the challenges that come with it. Her writing serves as a guide for those on their own journeys of growth, healing, and awakening, encouraging readers to embrace the highs and lows of life with grace and resilience.

INTRODUCTION
—◆—◆—◆—

Twin flame connections are often described as intense and transformative, marked by deep emotional and spiritual connections.

These relationships can feel like a mirror reflecting your innermost insecurities, fears, and desires, which is why they can be both exhilarating and challenging. The concept of twin flames suggests that the two souls are deeply connected, often going through cycles of separation and reunion to facilitate growth and healing. This process can be painful, as it forces both individuals to confront their deepest issues. The running and chasing dynamic is common in twin flame relationships because of the overwhelming intensity of the connection.

When one person is not ready to face these challenges, they may distance themselves to avoid the discomfort. As for the future of twin flames, it's believed that the ultimate goal is union, but this doesn't necessarily mean a romantic partnership in the traditional sense. Union can also signify a deep understanding and harmony between the two souls, even if they are not physically together. The journey is more about personal growth and spiritual evolution than simply being with another person. The idea of whether twin flames will ever stop mirroring insecurities depends on the individuals' willingness to face and heal their wounds. The process can take time and may involve several cycles of separation and reunion until both are ready to fully integrate the lessons learned.

The longing to be in the presence of a twin flame, to feel their touch, hear their voice, and experience that connection again, is a powerful emotion. It's essential to remember that this connection is also about finding that same love and wholeness within yourself. The twin flame journey is often seen as a path to self-discovery and unconditional love for oneself. Ultimately, whether twin flames have a future in this life depends on the individual journeys of the souls involved. It's about finding peace within yourself, knowing that the universe has a plan, and trusting in divine timing.

CHAPTER ONE

—♦—♦—♦—

Memoirs of my hometown

City life was never where I belonged. My heart has always been tied to the countryside, where the air is sweet and the rivers sing their endless songs. I spent countless afternoons on the riverbank, the sun gently warming my skin as I lost myself in the rhythm of the flowing water. Those were days of pure, unfiltered joy—leaping into the cool embrace of the river with my cousins, our laughter echoing as we splashed about, and our hands reaching into the clear water, hoping to catch the tiny guppies that darted around us.

Each time I walked the narrow dirt road back toward the farmhouse, I couldn't help but take mental pictures of the fields that seemed to stretch out forever, with the mountains watching over them from afar. My heart ached with the thought of leaving this place, knowing that in a few short months, I'd be trading it all for the unfamiliarity of the city. As I stepped through the white picket fence into the front yard, the intoxicating fragrance of flowers filled the air, and the birds sang from their perches in the mango trees. It was a scene so perfect, so full of life and beauty, that I wished I could freeze time and stay there forever, wrapped in the embrace of everything I knew and loved, instead of venturing into the unknown.

Beneath the sprawling canopy of the old mango tree, the world seemed to slow, offering moments of pure joy and simplicity. My hands would be full with mangoes, oranges, coconuts, and the sweetest berries, collected one by one from the abundant land that felt like an extension of myself. I would sit there with my cousins, who lived just next door, and together we would feast on nature's gifts, savoring the sweetness of both the fruit and the company.

There was work, too, but it never felt like a burden. After school, I'd help my grandparents in the vegetable patches, tending to the earth that gave so generously. We'd care for the horses, chickens, and ducks, their presence adding to the rhythm of life on the farm. Everything was alive, everything had a purpose, and so did I. But the city calls now, with its promise of new beginnings and different dreams.

As I prepare to leave, my heart aches for what I'll leave behind, especially my dog, Buddy. He was a free spirit, running wild and happy in the wide-open spaces of the farm. I can't imagine him cooped up in a city apartment, far from the fields where he belongs. So, I'll have to say goodbye, knowing that he'll be happier here, in the place that has always been our home.

I am Aniqua Travis, and this is the story of my life lived under open skies, surrounded by the love of family, the beauty of nature, and the memories that will forever be etched in my heart. I was a big girl now, I needed to get my life together. I had to move to a big city to get a job as a financial planner. The pay was great, but it just wasn't my type of lifestyle.

I longed for the freedom to set my own hours and build a business of my own, one that would allow me to work from anywhere in the world. But for now, I needed a job that would help me stand on my own, free from relying on my grandparents. More than anything, I dreamed of being able to support them as they grew older, giving back the care and love they had always shown me.

I have a strong desire to return home to live with my grandparents, who hold a special place in my heart. It would bring me great joy to have them visit me. I plan to take them on tours of the city and its surroundings. Obviously, moving away was challenging, but starting anew brought a sense of excitement. Fortunately, my friend Jess already resided in the same city, which provided me with a sense of comfort.

We often visited the beach, and as a coastal child, I always found solace and peace there. Every weekend was a sandy paradise, relishing both the sunrise and sunset. The serene evenings by the waves were magical, with shimmering stars and moonlit waters forming a captivating celestial display. I would linger until the coast was deserted, light a bonfire, and marvel at the stars.

The shooting stars never failed to provide a magnificent spectacle! The most enchanting nights were during a full moon, when I could witness the moon seemingly rising from the ocean, aglow.

Whenever my grandparents visited the city, they never stayed more than four days, as they had many animals waiting for them at home. While I understood their situation, it was always hard to see them leave. Returning to my small apartment, it felt empty, and I experienced loneliness. Sitting on my tiny balcony with a cup of coffee, I gazed at the city lights instead of the stars. The view was lovely, yet I felt nostalgic and homesick.

I noticed that I needed to cook healthier meals, as frozen food didn't match the deliciousness of my grandma's cooking. Therefore, I began watching recipe videos on YouTube every evening to enhance my cooking skills and make delicious meals.

Gradually improve my cooking skills. Over time, I not only learned how to prepare healthier meals, but I also started to rediscover the joy of cooking. Each dish brought back memories of my grandmother's kitchen and reminded me of the power of homemade food to nourish both body and soul. Cooking became more than just a necessity—it became a form of self-care and a creative outlet that I looked forward to every day.

After a year of apartment living in the city, I decided to relocate to the suburbs. City living wasn't for me as I felt suffocated due to my claustrophobia. I opted for a lovely cottage-style home with a spacious backyard, which was not only affordable but also provided a vegetable patch, fruit trees, and a charming flower garden. It's safe to say I've embraced a modern-day hippie lifestyle.

Guess I am a free spirit, outdoor-loving, butterfly-catching, sunbathing, adventure-seeking, mountain-climbing, beach-loving hippie at heart. I still do those things.

When I get a break from the grind, I have also realized that I have become a damaged human being with abandonment issues, and I don't even know how I got here.

I guess not having my mother by my side hurts a lot, but we all have issues, right? When I was 6 years old, my dad passed away in a car accident, so I never got the chance to really know him. Following his death, my mom struggled to cope with the loss of her life partner, turning to alcohol, which led to a downward spiral. For more than 20 years now, I have been living with my grandparents, which explains my strong emotional bond with them.

I visit my mom occasionally. She has remarried and started a new family. While she invited me to live with her, I preferred to stay with my grandparents, who have always been a constant support for me.

CHAPTER TWO

—◆—◆—◆—

Prince Charming, where art thou?

L ove has never been my forte. Perhaps I have yet to discover my so-called Prince Charming. I was unsure about the type of person I wanted in my life, the one who would sweep me off my feet unexpectedly – the love of my life. I guess I still believe in fairy tales. A guy full of joy, someone I could chat with endlessly without getting bored. His intense gaze sees right through to my soul.

His voice was like velvet, deep and husky, wrapping around me in a way that made my breath catch. My best friends Jess and Arisha kept me sane, and having girls' nights was something I would always look forward to.

One day, Jess came over after work so we could have dinner together. We always have so much to talk about. Jess's phone rang and she answered the call. I remember hearing a male voice and looking at her.

I smiled, raising an eyebrow as I playfully asked who was on the other end of the line. She leaned in and whispered that it was her cousin from back home. When she hung up, she turned to me with a grin and said he was moving to Australia.

A few moments later, her phone rang again as she headed to the bathroom. On a whim, I answered, feeling a flutter of excitement as if I were about to speak to a celebrity. My voice softened, and I took a deep breath before saying

8

hello, trying to keep my composure. I couldn't possibly admit to anyone that I was being ridiculous, feeling a connection to someone I didn't even know. But there was something there, something that made my heart skip, something that felt strangely significant.

A strange feeling of familiarity washed over me, one that I couldn't quite place. I've always had a sixth sense about things, but this was different—almost crazy. Naturally, I brushed it off. I simply told him that Jess would call him back soon.

But when I first heard his name mentioned in conversation, something in my heart stirred again. There was something about his name, something that felt like it was tethered to me, as if a part of me was inexplicably connected to it. It was just a common name, nothing out of the ordinary. Intuition, I suppose.

I tried to dismiss it, convincing myself it was nothing more than a passing thought. But deep down, an undeniable longing blossomed within me—a quiet yearning to meet this mysterious person, even though Jess had never mentioned his name. The thought of him lingered like a sweet, unspoken promise, tugging at my heart in a way that felt both strange and irresistibly beautiful.

Jess went to pick him up from the airport, and soon enough, he moved in with her. The first time I saw him, it was through the lounge room window. My breath caught in my throat as I watched him approach, and the only thought that raced through my mind was, *Oh my God, he's perfect. *

Suddenly, anxiety washed over me as I realized how long I had been staring, completely lost in his eyes. It hit me that I was still in my pajamas, my hair a tangled mess, and feeling the lingering effects of last night's party.

He walked right in front of me, and Jess introduced him to me. This is my cousin Alex, she said my eyes just twinkled, smiling softly. It was lunchtime, and I hurried to prepare something for both of them. As we talked, I couldn't help but notice how stunning Alex was. My eyes kept drifting toward him, and to my surprise, his gaze never left mine. The intensity of our eye contact sent shivers down my spine, and I suddenly realized that if Jess noticed, I'd be in serious trouble.

He only stayed for about an hour, but as he was leaving, still chatting with me, my heart skipped a beat. In that fleeting moment, I knew there was something between us, something undeniable that was only just beginning to take root. The connection was instant, and I had a feeling it was only going to grow from here.

It felt as though I had known him for a lifetime, though we had only met an hour ago. As I bid him farewell, my heart quietly longed for the moment our paths would cross again. The thought of the next gathering hosted by Jess filled me with a tender hope that he might be there.

Three months passed, and finally, an invitation arrived this time from Jess and Arisha, my other dear friends. My heart fluttered with the possibility of seeing Alex once more, and when he walked in, my breath caught. He was even more captivating than I remembered, his presence commanding in a ribbed black shirt that clung perfectly to his frame and dark blue jeans that accentuated his confident stride. His eyes sparkled with a warmth that drew me in, and in that moment, all the longing of the past months melted away.

I was completely overwhelmed. As he walked in, a spine-tingling buzz swept over me, sending waves of electricity through my entire body. It was as if just the sight of him had the power to stir something deep within me, something I couldn't ignore.

I couldn't deny it I had a crush on Alex. His eyes seemed to pierce right through me, as if he could see into my very soul. Curious and a little nervous, I asked Jess about him, and she mentioned he was a few years younger than me. I had never even considered dating someone younger—how was I supposed to start a conversation?

I could feel the warmth rising to my cheeks, certain I was blushing the entire time. But something about him stirred feelings in me that I had never experienced before. I knew I had to take a chance.

Gathering my courage, I walked over to him, my heart pounding. With a soft smile, I said, "Do you remember me? We met a few months ago—you came with Jess to my house." Alex's eyes sparkled with warmth as he gazed at me and said, "Of course I do. How could I ever forget a beautiful face like yours?" My heart soared, dancing with hope that maybe, just maybe, he felt something for me too.

Yet, a part of me wondered if he was simply being kind. As we chatted about work and life, I sipped on my mocktail, savoring the moment. Suddenly, he dropped a bombshell: he was starting a new job at the same company as Jess and me on Monday. My heart skipped a beat, and a wave of euphoria washed over me. It felt like fate had a hand in this. When his first day arrived, my excitement was palpable. During my lunch break,

I caught glimpses of him, and on this particular day, he wore a striking red shirt. It was a detail that made the day feel even more special, and I couldn't help but smile at the thought of our paths crossing more often.

I remember sitting at my laptop, focused on whatever was on the screen, when he came and stood next to me. The moment he got close, I caught the scent of his cologne—it was intoxicating, drawing me in like a magnet.

He leaned over me, asking me what I was working on, just enough to glance at the computer. I knew he did it on purpose. It felt like he somehow knew I had a crush on him, and he was enjoying the effect he had on me.

When he spoke, his voice low and close, I couldn't bring myself to meet his gaze. His eyes had this uncanny ability to pierce right through to my soul, and the intensity was almost too much to bear. Instead, I found myself looking anywhere but at him, hoping he wouldn't notice how completely he had unraveled me.

I soon realized that Alex had completely taken over my thoughts. Within a month, I had lost both my heart and my mind to him. All I wanted was to see Alex again.

It wasn't long before I noticed that I was asking Jess about his visits far too often, and she started to get suspicious. One day, she asked me directly, "Are you falling for him?" The smile that spread across my face was all the answer she needed. I couldn't hide anything from my best friends— they were like family to me. They knew every little detail about my life, even down to how I would react in certain situations. There was no keeping this secret from them; they could see right through me.

This could be dangerous if we ever had a falling out. If they ever let anything slip, I'd be in trouble. I always joked about how much we knew about each other, saying we could use it against one another. But deep down, I knew we had each other's backs no matter what. Despite the playful banter, our bond was unbreakable, and we would always support each other through everything life threw our way.

What was happening to me? My mind was swirling with more questions than answers, and sleep had become a distant memory. Desperate for clarity, I met up with my girls at our favorite coffee shop. As I took a quick sip of my cappuccino, I blurted out, "I can't take this anymore," trying to mask the overwhelming emotion in my eyes by looking away.

But they noticed something was off. Arisha leaned in, her curiosity piqued. "Spill the beans, girl. What's going on?" she urged. I hesitated, then finally looked up and whispered, "I think... I'm in love."

In that moment, I swear, their eyes grew three sizes bigger, filled with surprise and excitement. In unison, they both said, "Aww, honey, that's a good thing! Tell us, is it Alex?" I nodded, barely able to whisper, "Mmmm, yes." "Then why are you upset?" Jess asked, her brow furrowing in concern. "You should be happy you finally caught some feelings," Arisha chimed in, smiling. They teased me, saying they thought my heart had turned to stone from disuse, and we all burst into laughter.

But as the laughter faded, I softly confessed, quickly sipping my cappuccino to steady my nerves, "I'm so scared. I've never felt like this about anyone before." I confided in them that I was scared—what if he's just a player? I couldn't shake the way he kept glancing back at me all day. They reassured me, laughing as they said I was losing my mind along with my heart. We all shared a laugh, but their words stuck with me. Sleep on it," they suggested. "And if you still feel the same in the morning, face your fears. Take a leap and ask Alex if he'd like to grab a drink after work."

I couldn't help but wonder, though—did Alex realize how obvious he was being? Maybe he wanted me to fall for him. Maybe he loved the attention he was getting from me, but I couldn't take it anymore. finally, I got my courage up to ask or tell him that your eyes are piercing through to my heart and soul. I emailed him eeeekkk. I wanted to say

Please stop, stop looking at me that way. You are making me fall in love, but I didn't, as I had gone through so much with my ex.

Let's just say I was emotionally weak. I kept asking myself why would he ever want me, and he replied to my email, call me and I didn't because I was too scared he would reject me. I didn't want to get hurt again.

I was so flooded with oxytocin that my heart felt like it could stop from all the beats it skipped, day in and day out. The next day, we found ourselves working on a project together, with our manager right behind us, explaining something important. But I barely heard a word—because all I could do was stare into Alex's eyes, and he stared right back, like we were in a scene from a movie.

It was as if the world around us disappeared, and in that moment, our minds seemed to connect in a way words couldn't describe. Love was flowing between us in some invisible,

14

magical way. We were lost in another world, and for a heartbeat, I thought we might actually kiss. The intensity of our gaze was electric, and I could feel it deep in my soul.

I felt my heart leap, and a rush of panic overwhelmed me. In a moment of pure instinct, I found myself fleeing work, barely able to breathe, whispering that I wasn't feeling well and had to leave. My heart pounded in my chest, and I knew he could see the turmoil in my eyes the moment I stepped through the door. As soon as I got home, I fell to my knees, pleading with the heavens to take away these overpowering emotions that made me feel so utterly vulnerable.

But despite my prayers, the intensity between us only grew. Every time we were near each other, it was as if the world melted away, leaving just the two of us suspended in that electrifying tension. I vividly remember one day, walking into the room, and everything changed...

I saw that he was standing near the window near my desk, so I kept walking towards my desk, our eyes locked, he didn't move his eyes off me until Jess turned to see what he was looking at. she saw he was staring straight at me without even blinking, and when he did this, my eyes were glued in his direction until I sort of shook myself out of this. I used to get shy and not put my head up. I did see him flirting a few times with other colleagues, but never like this.

As I approached my desk, I noticed him standing by the window, his gaze fixed on me. Our eyes locked, and in that moment, it felt as if time stood still. He didn't look away, his intense stare holding me captive until Jess, curious, turned to see what had caught his attention. She noticed him watching me, unblinking, as if I were the only person in the room. I couldn't tear my eyes away from him, lost in the connection we shared, until I finally managed to pull myself back to reality. I used to be shy, rarely lifting my head, but this was different. Though I'd seen him flirt with others before, never had I felt this undeniable spark between us.

I couldn't take it any longer. I felt completely overwhelmed and unsure of what to do. The thought crossed my mind to email him, either to ask directly what he thought was happening between us or to bring up a casual topic that might naturally lead to the conversation I wanted to have. I just wanted to start a dialogue outside the office, hoping he might open up. Yet, part of me wondered—if he truly felt the same way, wouldn't he have made a move by now?

I can't believe I actually emailed him—who even does that? I have his number, so why didn't I just text him? Now I'm anxious as hell, overthinking everything. I barely slept that night. All I could replay in my mind was me typing, "Alex, I have something to tell you. Can you call me?"

CHAPTER THREE

—✦—✦—✦—

Trouble Trouble

I was like, oh shit I am in trouble!!! First phone conversation with him. The official one, anyway, was weird, yet I was so comfortable talking to him like I had known him for many years. It was weird, though, when Alex said that "I am a single man and I was just checking you out because you are too beautiful. "OKAY, I said, good to know. Inside my brain, I was like, ummmm AWKWARD.

I was so embarrassed that I had contacted Alex, as all this meant nothing to him, and I was already crazy about him. Talking to myself like a crazy person, "like really Anniqa, you just had to go embarrass yourself like that, you idiot." I thought I'd never contact him again, but Alex said "to keep in touch ". How could I not? Oh, I was so confused, and then a few hours later my phone rang. I saw a familiar number, and omg it was him, what did he want now, what's there to say, I am already feeling like shit. I answered nervously.

"Hey," I said softly. From the other end, I heard his deep, sexy reply: "Hey there. What are you up to?" That simple exchange marked the beginning of something extraordinary. I felt a swirl of emotions—anxious but thrilled, nervous yet undeniably excited. I knew this was the next step in a journey I never wanted to end.

From that moment on, our conversations grew longer and more meaningful, drawing us closer instead of apart. We began calling each other several times a day, sharing every detail of our lives, and opening up about our most intimate secrets. With every word, every story, I found myself falling deeper and deeper in love. He was everything I had ever dreamed of in a mankind, thoughtful, and so easy to talk to.

Two weeks later, Alex said, "Let's meet up for coffee." I didn't know if this would be the right thing to do, as it could possibly ruin our work relationship, but how could I not say yes? This man, over the last few weeks, has become my world, and he was the only one who ever made it go around. Anxiously willing to take a risk, I say yes.

He picked me up from home, and I got in the car and could not take my eyes off him. he just looked at me and smiled knowingly that I was in love or something, saying Hey, so where did you want to go?

We went to this Romantic European-style café with wooden chairs and tables, where the lights were all dimmed out and decorated with fairy lights, with dreamy, slow music to create the perfect mood. We both ordered cappuccinos and some churros, which were served with chocolate. yummy

While talking, we just kept looking into each other's eyes and then shying away, and suddenly he touched my hand to try to hold it. That was the first touch. Suddenly, tears rolled down my face, and I couldn't understand what was happening. Why the hell was I crying if he just held my hand, Oh, so embarrassing. What the hell was going through my mind, all I knew was I craved for this touch for ages, but not ages as this lifetime.

I was pulled to another lifetime. It felt like I found him who I was sent here to find. Yet I couldn't make sense of it, and I couldn't say these things to him out loud because if I did, he would think I was a psychopath and run in the other direction.

I knew then and there that there was something more than just a normal connection. I felt this overwhelming happiness, undeniable feelings like I was dying inside for his touch for centuries. He was even more confused than I was. He asked if I was ok, and he asked, "Did I do something wrong? I am sorry if I did." I said no, and I didn't even understand why was that happening. We decided to leave the cafe and go for a drive, maybe park somewhere quiet to understand what was really going on.

On the drive, I spoke to Alex like he was my best friend for years. We laughed at each other's jokes and shared stories. We stopped near a lake surrounded by birds and trees with green leaves and vines hanging from it, swaying every time the wind blew and the moon shone into the lake, leaving a shadow.

He looked into my eyes as I looked away, smiling. He asked if I was ok and what was really going on. I explained that I wasn't sure why I was emotional. Nothing was making sense, as this had never happened before. Alex said "Enough" as he grabbed me and kissed me with passion, looking straight into my eyes intensely like I was a mirror,

In that moment, it felt as though our souls had reunited, igniting a love that had been waiting for eternity. I was breathless, completely overwhelmed, as tears began streaming down my face, beyond my control.

He looked at me, confused by my sudden wave of emotion. I had never cried because of a touch or a kiss before, but this was different. This wasn't just a kiss—it was the realization that I had finally found the one I had been searching for my entire life. I gazed into his eyes, my voice trembling as I whispered, "Kiss me again."

Without hesitation, he leaned in, his lips meeting mine once more. A shiver coursed through me, lighting up every nerve in my body. My eyes locked onto his, unable to look away, as his soft lips sent me into heaven I'd never known.

But even in that perfect moment, I gently pulled away, my heart racing, knowing this was just the beginning of something eternal. As he tilted his head and asked, Are you ok? I replied with ahahh. We decided that we were going to take a walk on the beautiful lake gardens. We were just on the same level, we understood each other's quirky jokes and sudden feeling of fulfillment as if I could do this all my life with him.

I didn't even want to go back home, but obviously I had to, but as soon as he dropped me off, we were back on the phone. Things were getting heated between us, and we couldn't resist each other even at work, a quick peck on the lips. Here and there, when no one was watching, we'd steal quiet moments together. We weren't ready for anyone at work to know about us yet; it would have made things awkward.

Of course, my girls knew. They were my confidantes, the ones I could pour my heart out to about everything, especially the way tears had rolled down my face the first time he touched me. It was impossible to explain, but they understood. We'd sneak messages to each other, planning quick, stolen kisses in the work restroom, and later laugh about how ridiculous it all was.

The most intoxicating part, though, was the way we felt every time we were near each other. It was like we'd just shared half a bottle of wine—light-headed, giddy, and completely swept away by the high of being together. And the funniest part? Neither of us drank. It was just us, and it was addictive in the best way.

Drunk in love, yes, it's real. I could see him everywhere. I dropped him home, as i was leaving, he turned around and looked at me, and in my head, it felt like he felt the same about me, and one night, he told me that I was perfect for him in every way. He told me that the first day he saw me, he was in awe.

When I actually looked like shit and was in my pj's. I was in dreamland, was he really saying this?? I really did look like a mess when he saw me the first day. In a whisper, I said Alex, I love you and he replied I love you too.

Unreal, I couldn't believe this; I was over the moon. Jumping around the house like someone just gave me a million dollars.

CHAPTER FOUR

—✦—✦—✦—

Is he going away for good?

Alex came from an orthodox Catholic family, deeply rooted in tradition and strict in their beliefs. He had shared bits and pieces about their way of life, the expectations placed on him, and the values they held close. While he never seemed overly burdened by it, I could sense the weight of those traditions lingering in the background of his life.

It was only a few months into our relationship when Alex called me, his voice heavy with worry. He explained that he had to return to the Greek islands immediately—his aunt Tana had suffered a heart attack, and her condition was serious.

The news hit me hard. I knew how much Aunt Tana meant to him. She wasn't just an aunt; she was the one who had raised him, shaping him into the man he was. His love and respect for her were evident in every story he told, in the way he spoke of her with warmth and admiration. I could feel the depth of his concern through the phone, and my heart ached for him.

But as much as I was worried for her health and for Alex's emotional state, another fear began to creep into my mind. What if his family saw this as an opportunity to push him into something he didn't want? What if they used this moment to convince him to settle down with someone from their community?

The thought of him being pressured into an arranged marriage sent a pang of anxiety through me. I tried to push those thoughts aside, reminding myself to focus on what mattered most—his aunt's recovery and being there for Alex in whatever way he needed. But deep down, the worry lingered.

I couldn't shake the fear that the very traditions and expectations he had grown up with might pull him away from me, and I wasn't sure how to stop that from happening. As I hung up the phone, I sat there for a moment, staring at nothing, caught in the whirlwind of emotions. I wanted to be strong for him, to support him through this difficult time, but I couldn't ignore the tiny voice in the back of my mind whispering, what if you lose him?

His aunt Tana was sick, and she always wanted to see Alex getting married. a fear of losing him overtook me, but I tried to stay strong as I dropped him off at the airport. He leaned over and kissed me like it was goodbye. Looking straight into my eyes, he stops and says I'll be back soon, take care of yourself and walks out, driving back, trying to assess the situation. I knew that we were both wrong in getting so close, yet it felt so right.

I could not sleep that night waiting to hear from him. I fell asleep with the phone still in my hand. It must have been late. My phone rang at 4.30 in the morning. I jumped up and picked up the call. Alex told me that his trip was exhausting, and he hasn't even gotten out of the plane yet. I was so overwhelmed to hear from him, but it was beyond words to explain how I felt knowing he had called men before he got off the plane.

I didn't hear from Alex for like 2 days because he didn't have a local SIM or even an internet connection, but he had already warned me of this earlier. so I waited and waited hours seemed like days but finally my phone rang and a hunky male voice said hey babe sorry I had no phone sim for the last few days and that's why I couldn't contact you, how have you been I've missed you so much, breathless from hearing his voice after so long I could hardly take words out of my mouth,

I heard myself saying I am so glad you called. I missed you, too. We spoke for about 5 minutes when I heard a female voice calling him. he said he would call back as soon as he could. He had a lot of families over for lunch, days turned into weeks, and he didn't seem like he was going back anytime soon.

We spoke every day for at least an hour. One day, I asked Alex if he had spoken about us to his family. Alex said no but he will soon, a few more weeks past and his aunt Tana was much better now so I asked him again saying babe I feel like I can't live without you please try and talk to your family about me, Alex suddenly said he did already and they refused to have me in their family because I would not understand their culture and background. I was stunned and shocked at what he was telling me. He said, "his family has arranged for him to get married to another girl from the same background as him. I couldn't believe what I was hearing him say.

I lost it and started arguing, saying, "Why would they say that. Does your family know that we love each other?" and his reply killed me when he said his family's happiness is more

24

important to him than his own, or was he saying this just so he could get rid of me? He cut me off and started talking to me in a higher tone than his normal.

He told me that when he comes back, he will go and meet the girl that his family arranged, and we can no longer be together. I went into shock, but I wasn't able to say then why did you lead me on. Please understand that it is not possible for us to be together, and this is goodbye."

I stood there with my phone still in my hands, shocked at what had just happened. We wanted to spend our lives together, and this was so unexpected, tears running down my face, feeling betrayed, and thinking, was it he that didn't really want me?

Why didn't he fight to be with me? How could he just let me go, just like that? How could it really be over, breaking down and falling down on the ground, crying my heart out? I felt this unexplainable pain like someone had just died. Was it me, or was I mourning a relationship that I assumed was my happily ever after? Days turned into weeks, and still he hadn't called or replied back to me. I had sent like a million emails begging and begging to not do this to me, I didn't want to lose him.

I missed him so much. I cried. I saw his pic and started kissing and hugging it like a crazy person, I couldn't understand how he could be like this. I thought I knew him. It had been 2 weeks since he told me that he didn't want anything to do with me. I emailed to ask how he was and he replied that he was back here in Australia and that he wanted to see me, I was in shocked and not once did I think, NO, this guy just broke my heart, I should not go see him, I sat in my car and drove straight to him, it was like nothing ever happened.

I sat next to him, and he pretended like he didn't break my heart. He moved forward to kiss, I backed up then realizing that I couldn't go through the pain again but he moved in again to kiss and I could not stop myself, I was dying to have his touch the connection the passion his love I just felt complete in that moment, he hugged me like he had missed me so much but not a word uttered.

He just held me in his arms, and I felt whole again. My love was back. I didn't talk about what had happened a few weeks ago and how we broke up. We started chatting again every day like nothing ever happened, we are in love, just like before, until one day I messaged him when he got home, and there was no reply. He has started talking to other girls, I told myself. Alex told me that he was going to go meet his so-called fiancée, which broke me down.

I was confused about why he was kissing me and meeting up with me when he knew he had a fiancée. He told me that he is going to meet her in Melbourne, where she lives, and that I shouldn't message him for 3 days when he's there. He said this is what his family wants, and he has no stan. The first thing I ask is, will you be staying with her? He told me he was staying with an old friend, but he would go see her to see if they were even compatible.

I was filled with sorrow. I couldn't even get out of bed for 3 days straight. I became a vegetable; I just couldn't deal with the pain. I felt betrayed, but I had no say in this. Thankfully, Jess and Arisha came around and made me get up and fix myself up as well as make me laugh. These girls breathe life back into me. I saw pictures of Alex in a new city with his fiancée on Facebook.

Broken, I chucked my phone and started bawling my eyes out that my story with him was now over. I love him, and I will pray every day to make me stop loving him so much. Make me stop because it was painful, knowing that he didn't care that I cared. He never loved me like I loved him, I thought to myself. I just wanted one thing for Alex to be happy wherever he is.

We had been broken up for 2 weeks and 3 days. Yes, I was counting every single day that I survived through the pain that my love put me through. I was in denial. no doubt. I think this may be our official breakup, I thought to myself. we will never get back together ever again. I am very heartbroken and feel like I have lost something so precious to me. Tears were running down my face. I wish I could just hug Alex one more time. Jess and Arisha were by my side,

I just want to talk to him one more time. I need closure. I had realized that everything was apparently my fault in this relationship, or maybe he just made it out that way. He's a narcissist. I can't believe that this was even a topic. In my eyes, my love for him was a union of two souls, two hearts that combined into one, but as I said, it is my side of the story. Alex obviously saw things differently.

One day, I randomly opened my email, and Alex had emailed me saying he had broken up with his fiancée because they were too different, and he wanted to see me, like an idiot in love, I succumbed and replied. He came over to see me. I was mad still, but he kept hugging me and cuddling me, and that made me forget every pain I had felt for those moments. I made dinner for the two of us. He was cuddling me from behind the whole time.

I was making dinner, and once in a while, he would turn me around to kiss my lips ever so gently. I melted faster, like the butter on the heat. After dinner, we decided to watch a movie all cuddled up with a blanket. The movie wasn't finished when he said Let's go upstairs. I asked if he was sleepy because I was finding the movie interesting, but he wasn't. oh well, I thought. Upstairs sounds good, wink wink. As soon as I stood up, he just picked me up like a baby. I kept saying Oh my god, I am going to fall but he reassured me with Don't worry, I won't let you fall.

A sudden sense of security and safety overtook my heart, knowing that he won't let me fall. He took me to the room and put me on the bed. He started kissing me deeply, his eyes locked into mine. Oh, I had music playing in my head, some romantic song I can't even remember. I was just lost in that moment, feeling the love.

He began gently unbuttoning my top, his movements slow and deliberate. I didn't want him to stop. When we finally made it to the bed, it felt like our bodies were merging — two souls finally finding their way back to each other. I was in his arms, wrapped in a moment that felt like magic, like everything I had ever waited for was happening right then.

He hovered over me, his eyes locked with mine, and asked softly, "Can I?" My heart skipped. Did he really just ask me that? No one had ever made me feel so seen, so desired not just physically, but deeply. I looked at him, completely in awe, and without a word, I gave him my answer.

And in that moment, we made the most beautiful, soul-stirring love. It was all fireworks after that. I drifted off in his arms, his steady heartbeat lulling me into the deepest, most peaceful sleep I'd had in years.

Wrapped in his warmth, it felt like heaven, like the world had melted away and left only us in our little cocoon of bliss. The soft morning light poured through the curtains, and I woke up to find him still fast asleep, his face serene, lips slightly parted, his arm gently draped over me. For a moment, I just watched him, my heart full. How did I get so lucky? He looked like a dream, untouched by worry, glowing in the gentle sunlight.

I slipped out of bed and tiptoed to the bathroom, letting the warm water cascade over me, trying to ground myself in the reality of it all. Suddenly, through the hum of the shower, I heard his sleepy, low voice call out, "Can I join you?" Caught off guard, I felt a flutter of nerves. Daylight meant exposure— every curve, every flaw. But something in his tone, soft yet full of desire, gave me courage. "Yes," I whispered, almost breathlessly.

He stepped in behind me, the sunlight streaming through the frosted glass casting golden rays across his skin. I turned slightly and smirked, teasing, "Looks like the morning sun is up…" My eyes sparkled with mischief. Before I could finish my thought, he pressed me gently but firmly against the warm, tiled wall. The steam curled around us like a secret, cloaking our bodies in heat and haze. His hands explored my waist as his lips trailed along my neck, igniting sparks along my skin. Every kiss was a promise, every touch a confession of how deeply he desired me.

The air between us thickened with intimacy, not just of bodies, but of hearts opening up in the silence. In that moment, time stood still—two souls tangled beneath falling water and rising passion, held together by more than just physical heat. It was tender, intense, and beautifully raw.

The very next day, it was his birthday, and I was so excited. I said to him, Let's go out and celebrate, but he said No, I don't feel like it. I was like, okay, then I'll come see you, and he said no. I was shocked at what he was saying. he said he needed to be alone, and he broke up with me again, and that's on his birthday, which I wanted to make so special.

I wanted everything to be perfect. Again, he was pushing me away. Was he talking to other girls? I sat there thinking, all this was driving me insane. I wanted to be with him—truly be with him. My heart was all in, wrapped around every word he said, every glance he gave me, every fleeting moment we shared. But he kept using me... and pushing me away whenever it suited him. It was like he had me on a string, tugging when he was lonely or bored, and dropping me when he didn't need me anymore. And the worst part? He knew. He knew exactly how naïve I was, how deeply and madly in love I had

It shattered me. I couldn't understand how he moved on so quickly. How he gave someone else the words I had begged to hear, the love I had hoped for, the commitment I thought we were building toward. It felt like a slap to the face... like everything I had given him—my time, my heart, my vulnerability- was tossed aside as if it were worthless.

I wasn't just heartbroken. I was humiliated, confused, and utterly lost. And still, a part of me kept hoping he'd come back, even when every part of me knew I deserved more. Alex doesn't even seem like the same person I fell in love with. I started seeing dreams of him getting married to someone. Was he really married to someone already? I didn't know what was going on.

I can't believe what he says that he has someone else in his life, ahh, the guts he had. All I wanted to do was swear at him for treating me like I was nothing, but the fear of losing him forever would make me shut up. I told myself I just feel lucky that he still lets me see him. My standards were gone; I no longer had any boundaries left because I loved a player.

I succumbed to being a side chick. I felt trapped, like I had no choice in this. I was a toy he played with and threw me away when he got bored, or was it something else? he was trying to find a life partner that his family was happy with. I had lost control of my life, as well as my sanity and everything in between. He would say come see me and I would run. We would make love, then talk for a week, and again he would say no more.

He once told me that he didn't want to get close because he really doesn't want to develop any more feelings because there is no future, but every now and then he would randomly reply to my I love you So, by now I was sure that he loved me but was trying to stay away. Months turned into years, and I learned to block him, too, but then he would call Jess and Arisha and ask them to pass a message to me.

31

I would instantly unblock him, and we would end up seeing each other that week, and then a week will pass, and he will block me again. I have no one to blame but myself for allowing this to go on for so long. I am still madly in love with Alex, and I know I don't get to see him as often as I would like to. If he were my boyfriend, I guess that wouldn't be the case. We would be able to see each other whenever we wanted to, but I can't seem to be able to move on without him, and because he keeps coming back.

He makes me feel truly loved, even if I only get to see him once every few months. Time with him is rare, but when we're together, it's intense, comforting, and real. I feel completely his—emotionally, physically, and spiritually. And even when he's gone, there's a part of me that stays connected to him. The separation hurts more than I can explain, but somehow, I still hold on, because what I feel for him is so deep and consuming.

We are alike in ways that sometimes make things complicated. Our pride, our egos, our stubbornness—they mirror each other so much that it's like looking into a reflection. He's strong, but I know he carries a sense of duty to his family. He doesn't want to upset his parents or go against their expectations. I understand that, but it still hurts to be kept in the shadows because of it.

What we have sometimes feels dangerously close to being labeled as just a "casual thing," a relationship based mostly on physical connection. That's the thin line we keep walking. And yet, for me, it's never been casual. He told me he couldn't give me more, and that crushed me. Because I wasn't asking for everything—I was just asking for honesty, commitment, and maybe a little hope.

The confusing part is how natural it all feels when I'm with him. Every time I've hugged him, there's been this strange, powerful feeling inside me—almost like a voice whispering in my heart, "This is your husband." I've been shocked by how clearly I've heard it, like it wasn't just a thought but a message. It's happened more than once, and each time it made me pause. What is this connection? Why does it feel so destined?

I don't know what he felt in those moments. Maybe he never felt the same. I was so telepathically connected to him. I knew he was thinking about me, and he was going to message me very soon. I was getting tired of this type of relationship. I wanted commitment. I wanted to know he was mine. I finally decided to ask Grandma. I went to see my Grandma. I told her who Alex was and how he used to disappear on me for months at a time. I was very close to her since I was a child, I was able to tell her everything, and I knew she would always give me good advice. I didn't want to stress her out; I knew she would start worrying about me.

I needed her advice as she was so wise. She told me he can only treat you this way because you allow it. Stop it, she said, raise your standards, and he will need to comply, and if he has true feelings, he will even ask for your hand in marriage.

CHAPTER FIVE

—◆—◆—◆—

Putting my foot down

Finally, I got my courage up to call Alex. I told him, I can no longer do this, no relationship……. relationship with him. I felt stronger already just by uttering these words. He went quiet for a few seconds, and then he said, 'Let's have a last break-up party.' I said 'no no no no no no but he persuaded me. One last time, I thought. I can't blame him.

I would have liked to see him one last time, too. The truth is, I didn't know how long we would last in this breakup situation because he had broken up many times before. He said he will come see me in like 2 hours because he was still at work.

I can't describe how I felt every time I saw him. As soon as I would hear a knock on the door, my heart would start racing, I would take a couple of seconds to compose myself before opening the door, as he walked in, he would give me a peck on my lips, then he hugged me, even a hug that made me feel like

I was his world, and sometimes while I was hugging him, he would pick me up and take me to the sofa in the living room. We would sit and just chat, and as boring as that sounds, it was so fulfilling. I would make dinner for both of us before he came to see me so that we could sit and chat at the dinner table.

I would go into the kitchen, and when he wasn't looking, I would jump around with happiness. Like that's how emotionally fulfilled I was spending time with him. He was like a drug to me. I was addicted to him, his presence, his essence, his love, his touch, his hugs, his smile, and his face.

He would let me sit on his lap, and I would say close your eyes. I want to take pictures of you with my eyes, and I would look at you to my heart's content. I suddenly realized that, omg, I can't live without this man, and I was about to break up with him. Am I serious? Like really, will I be able to go through this? This was a bad idea, a terrible idea actually.

Do I really want to do this? Anxiety started hitting fast. As he kissed me, looking into my eyes, I heard him whisper I love you. And instantly, I replied I love you, too. Ahhhhh, it's a trap to keep me wrapped around his fingers. He knows this way; I won't be able to leave. I am sure I will suffer more without seeing him than he will. I hope I don't start running after him this time round.

I missed him so deeply that I reached out—just a simple email to ask how he was, hoping for some kind of response, even a few words. But there was nothing. No reply. The silence hurt more than I expected. It made me feel lost, invisible, and broken in a way I can't quite describe.

Without him, it's like a part of me is constantly aching. I've tried to be strong, to move on, but the emotions keep pulling me back. So I find myself praying—over and over again—just asking God to take these feelings away, to help me let go, to bring me peace because holding on is starting to hurt more than I can bear.

I keep thinking time will heal, but it's not happening. I dream about him every night and wake up in love with Alex every day. I have started to see dreams of things that have never happened in this lifetime. I know it sounds really stupid and bizarre, but it feels like I have known him from a life before, or something, can it be?

I made an appointment to see a past life regression therapist, who is well known for getting to the inner memoirs of the soul. I had heard that after a regression session, many people discovered the roots of their strange behaviors and deep obsessions. It intrigued me. By that time, it had been seven months since I'd last seen Alex. Surprisingly, I was feeling emotionally stronger than ever—like I had finally reached a place where I could love him without needing him in my life. I no longer felt attached to whether he was present or not. His absence no longer defined my emotional state.

I remember telling Jess that I hadn't felt this emotionally grounded in the entire four years since I met Alex. For the first time, I felt like I had reclaimed my power. Out of curiosity, I decided to visit a regressionist. I wasn't expecting much. I didn't even really believe in past lives—it always seemed like a far-off concept.

But something inside me nudged me to explore it, just to see if anything meaningful might come to the surface. As I walked in, I was greeted by a woman who instantly put me at ease—she had this calm, radiant energy that made me feel safe. I told myself, whatever comes out of this experience, I'll take it with an open heart.

I explained to her right away that I was skeptical about the whole thing, but I was willing to give it a try, especially since she came highly recommended by my best friend. She led me into a quiet, softly lit room. I lay down on a comfortable bed, surrounded by the gentle hum of meditation music playing in the background. The air was filled with the soothing scent of lavender, which made the atmosphere feel peaceful and grounding.

She asked me to close my eyes and gently guided me to focus on her voice. "Just follow my instructions," she said. Her voice was calm and steady. "Go deeper and deeper into your thoughts." With each word, I felt myself slipping further from the noise of everyday life and more into the quiet corners of my mind.

As the session went on, I reached a point where I wasn't fully aware of what I was saying. It felt like I was somewhere in between dreaming and waking, present, yet far away. Afterward, I remembered fragments, but not everything. She filled in the gaps for me, gently recounting what had unfolded during the session. What I remembered most clearly was the overwhelming wave of emotion—I cried so much. It was like something deep inside me had finally been given a voice.

She told me that sometimes people need multiple sessions to reach that level of release, but with me, everything just came pouring out. I was both nervous and excited to know what really happened—what I had said, what surfaced from within me. And then she told me something unexpected: she had recorded the entire session. My heart raced. I couldn't believe it—there was a recording.

I was about to hear myself speak truths I didn't even know I'd been carrying. Listening to that recording was a life-changing experience. I played it back over and over, each time feeling a wave of disbelief wash over me. I couldn't believe the words that were coming out of my own mouth. It felt like I was hearing someone else speak—someone from a distant time, yet unmistakably me.

I started crying as I listened. Over and over, I repeated, "He fell... he died." The grief in my voice was raw, haunting. "He left me here all alone to raise our kids," I said through sobs. Wait—kids? That stunned me. I had never imagined children in this life with him, yet there I was, in the session, speaking of them as if they were real, as if I had lived and loved them.

She gently asked me their names, and even in my distressed state, I answered without hesitation: "Regina and Samuel." Then she asked, "What do you see in front of you?" And I said, "It's my husband... he has blood coming from his face." The words shook me to my core. It wasn't just imagination—it felt like a memory buried in my soul, surfacing for the first time. I could feel the pain, the loss, the heartbreak of that moment like it had happened yesterday.

I was shaking my husband's chest, but he was lying there lifeless. She said Now go back further to the start, where do you live. It looked like a dusty village all around me. I saw we were on a bicycle and a house that looked like it was about to fall apart. A small shack. I saw a tree in my yard under which people were sitting. There were ladies under the tree, but I saw myself there with an unrecognizable face, but I knew it was me. These were very similar to my dreams. I was holding a baby girl, and I kept calling her Regina.

38

Regina: I recognized that name from a previous dream I had when we were on a beach, and I called out to my daughter Regina. That's the same name I got again. She asked me to go to a time with my husband, and the scene changed. We were inside the house, and he was making tattoos on my back.

It was some kind of writing, possibly a language that I didn't know. I felt so much love for him; I recognized him this time, and it was my heart and soul. The love of my life, Alex. I was shaking. His face didn't look the same. There was a way too heavy beard on his face, but it was him. I didn't believe all that I heard and what I saw through the regression. It does explain my obsessions with Alex and why I am always scared to lose him. Anyways, the regressionist advised that you will still get parts and parts of the past coming back now until we finish off and close off all memories.

I was so astounded at what I had found out that afternoon that I called Alex and asked him to come over for dinner, and he actually said yes to me. That night, as we sat and ate, I didn't tell him anything about what I found out from the past life regression, as it was too weird to comprehend between us.

I saw him in a different light. I remembered how, when I saw him the very first time, I felt this instant connection of knowing him; over the years, I hugged him and felt my soul scream out that this was my husband. How we have the same birthmarks and even the same father's names, my fears of losing this man, it all just made sense like we were meant to find each other again, but if the regression was true, then why didn't he recognize me or my soul? Why did he treat me this way? Where was the real love of a lifetime together?

That night, I was sitting on his lap like I usually did, facing him. I told him to close his eyes so I could take mental pictures of him for the time we would be apart, so I could remember his beautiful face whenever I closed my eyes, and like always, he smiled and closed his eyes. After a few minutes of losing myself within him, I just cuddled him. He playfully squeezed me so hard I screamed. We looked into each other's eyes, and I whispered I love you. There was no reply. He just pulled me closer and put his lips on mine. He waited for me to resist, but I didn't.

He kissed me slowly, like he meant it. If there was a haven on earth feeling, this was it. My eyes just rolled back into my head for those minutes as I opened my eyes. I saw him looking straight into my eyes. Eyes are truly the window to the soul. I have seen and felt it.

Who was I kidding? I was still madly in love with him. I need to stop lying to myself. Things got a bit heated, and I got up to pull his arm and direct him to come upstairs. Every ounce of me was thanking god for bringing him into my life; otherwise, I wouldn't know what love felt like.

I still couldn't believe I was with him. We made love all night long. he held me so close as we fell asleep; I could hear him breathing, my heart crying, don't let me go. A Gentle peck on the cheek before holding me close again in his sleep.

Holding my hand fingers locked, I felt like I was a lost child who needed the comfort of his touch and guidance. Hugging so tightly and hearing his heartbeat and touching his skin, letting him know with my touch how much I have missed him. He woke up early and said he needed to go as he started work soon. He stepped out of the shower, water still glistening on his skin, a towel wrapped low around his waist.

For a moment, I just lay there watching him—he looked breathtaking, like something out of a dream. My lips curled into a soft smile. I wanted to pull him back into bed, to hold onto just a little more time with him, but I knew he had to leave. He leaned over and kissed me—just a gentle touch of lips, unmoving, delicate. Then, a playful bite.

That single spark shifted everything. The kiss deepened, becoming slow and passionate, charged with everything we weren't saying. "I love you," I heard myself whisper, almost involuntarily, as I reached up to hold his face, my fingers running through his damp hair. But he caught both my hands and gently pinned them down, eyes locked with mine as if to say, kiss me, but don't touch. Always teasing. Always leaving me wanting more. And at that moment, with my heart racing and his lips so close, all I wanted was to kiss him again—and never stop.

I just prayed that I wasn't reading him wrong. I felt it within my soul and every ounce of my being; maybe that's my rose-colored glasses, but something made me feel that this was my prince charming, just without the horse. Is he here to save me from the burning castle of doom or to shred my heart to bits? Don't know which one it will be. I got up to give him a hug and goodbye. We hugged for several minutes until my heart's content. My soul screamed out My hubby, please don't leave me; you are my everything.

Like, what the hell. One side of me is jumping with joy, the other is like a friend, really!!! Are you serious??? A Baby with him?? Friends forever?? WTF Anyway, I was still ok with that as he wasn't someone who shared much of his feelings very often, so this was progress, I guess.

This time, he wasn't running. We started seeing each other every week, and it was just amazing. Spending time with him is all I wanted, without him pushing me away. It was almost his birthday, and I suggested that we go on a holiday.

We decided to go to Bali. I have always loved taking holidays but never with anyone. Lone traveler I was. For the first time I was going to have company, he said yes, I cannot believe this. I have suggested it before, but he always said no, but he also loves traveling.

Alex has traveled extensively. We started planning our trip, but he wasn't going to join me for the first few days as he was still working and couldn't take time off. We planned where we would stay.

What are you going to do there? I am a planner, so I like to look at all the activities and books.in advance was an exciting time. I never ever got this much time with him. I told my grandparents that I would be back in 2 weeks and that I was going with friends.

I arrived in Bail, oh what a beautiful country. The weather was warm, and the wind was always blowing warmer, but I loved warmer weather; it was just my thing. The very next day, I drove out to a beach that I heard was pretty much isolated. I don't like very crowded places. The beach was pure magic—like something straight out of a travel commercial. The water shimmered in clear shades of green, the sand was a warm, golden stretch of perfection, and best of all, it was almost completely untouched by crowds.

I wandered barefoot along the shore, the fine sand slipping between my toes. The wind played with my hair as I strolled along the water's edge, lost in a state of calm. It felt meditative—so peaceful, so grounding. I ended up sitting there for hours, just soaking it all in.

Eventually, Alex called. I turned on the video to show him the breathtaking view. He smiled and said he couldn't wait to join me—and jokingly told me not to visit all the good places without him. We both laughed, and in that moment, everything felt just right.

I was driving back to my hotel with the music turned all the way up—just so I could sing along. I'm not much of a singer, which is exactly why I cranked the volume. I didn't want anyone to hear me. I was flying down the road at over 100 kilometers per hour, stopping every now and then to snap photos of the picturesque villages I passed along the way.

The next morning, I headed to the hotel lobby to grab a coffee. That's when I met Larisa, who happened to be from Australia too. We struck up a conversation, and she started telling me about some stunning spots in the area. She mentioned she was heading out for a walk and asked if I'd like to join her.

I smiled and said, "Yes, please!"—excited at the thought of exploring with someone new. Larisa told me to meet her in the lobby in 30 minutes. Right on time, I met her there, and we set off on a long, beautiful walk to the gorge. The river flowed over smooth rocks, and peacocks roamed freely through the park, adding a touch of magic to the scenery. We even crossed a wobbly suspension bridge and took a thrilling chair ride over the landscape.

Larisa and I instantly connected. It was like meeting a kindred spirit—we were so alike in so many ways. We ended up spending the entire day together, laughing, sharing stories, and soaking in the beauty around us. The day before he arrived, I went out shopping for the both of us. I was full of anticipation and joy—I could hardly wait for our journey to begin. He was arriving at midday, and my heart was already racing with excitement.

Before he arrived, I stood at the airport, waiting—nervous energy coursing through me. My hands were shaking, and I could feel a full- blown panic attack coming on. Yes, I struggled with anxiety, and in that moment, it was hard to tell if it was fear or excitement. I kept whispering to myself, You're safe. You're okay. This is just excitement.

Then, I saw him. As he walked out of the terminal toward me, my heart raced. The moment our eyes met, I felt a chill run down my spine—an electric mix of joy, relief, and anticipation. He had driven all the way to Tejakula—a hidden gem nestled between the mountains and the sea. The landscape was breathtaking. Towering peaks embraced the quiet town, and the ocean shimmered so close by, it felt like the edge of the world.

What a beautiful place to be "trapped" in—with the most handsome man my eyes had ever seen. I could hardly contain myself. My breathing was still heavy, my heartbeat racing, as we cruised down the nearly empty highway. My eyes kept drifting to him, unable to look away. Every now and then, he'd glance at me, smile, and my whole body would melt.

We sang along to songs the entire way, windows down, the wind mixing with our laughter. When we finally arrived at the hotel, I silently thanked the universe—it was perfect. The room opened up to a stunning view of the ocean, with the sound of waves softly crashing in the background. We were only staying for one night before starting our tour, but even in that short time, everything already felt unforgettable.

We were both starving, so we decided to head out for dinner. Sitting across from him at the restaurant, it suddenly hit me—this was our first real date. Just the two of us. My heart swelled with a strange mix of joy and sorrow. All those years of knowing him, and somehow, life had never given us this simple moment: two people, one table, no distractions. It had always been group dinners—his friends, my friends, family gatherings—but never us.

As he reached across the table and gently held my hand, I felt something shift inside me. My eyes welled up, and before I could stop them, tears rolled down my cheeks. Concerned, he handed me a serviette and softly asked, "Is everything okay?" I nodded, smiling through the tears. "Yes," I whispered. "More than okay." I felt overwhelmed as I looked at him, my voice barely steady. "You know... this is our first official date." He smiled, a little surprised. "Oh yeah, it is!" Then, noticing the tears in my eyes, he added, "You should be happy—why are you crying?" I gave him a soft smirk, brushing away a tear. "These are tears of joy."

I had never felt like this about anyone. Ever. I couldn't take my eyes off him. Later that night, as he lay asleep beside me, I found myself just... staring. Admiring. Completely captivated. It felt surreal—amazing, even—to know that when he woke up, he wouldn't be leaving. He was here with me.

He slept so peacefully, while I lay wide awake, buzzing with excitement, unable to close my eyes. I watched the rise and fall of his chest, the calm on his face. Thank God he doesn't snore, I thought, smiling to myself. I woke up early and went for a walk to catch the sunrise at the beach—my favorite part of the day. The world felt still, peaceful, and full of promise.

I sat quietly on the sand, watching as the first golden light broke over the horizon, painting the sky in soft pinks and oranges. I couldn't help but take a few pictures, trying to capture the beauty that felt like a direct gift from God. Every holiday I've ever taken has included moments like this—watching the sun rise and set. Even at home, I can see the sunrise from my bedroom window, but I cannot hear the sound of the ocean in the morning. That's something else entirely. It's a kind of peace you can't put into words.

Feeling thankful, I made my way back to the hotel, stopping to pick up breakfast and coffee for the both of us. A perfect start to another unforgettable day. When I got back to the hotel, he was still fast asleep. I smiled, placed the breakfast beside him, and said softly, "Wake up, sleepyhead." He stirred, rubbing his eyes, and looked at me in surprise. "Where did you go off to?" "I went down to the beach to watch the sunrise," I said, handing him a coffee. "Picked up breakfast on the way back for us."

He sat up, touched by the gesture. "You should've woken me. I would've gone with you." We had breakfast in bed, the morning light pouring in through the windows, the ocean murmuring in the distance. We lay there for a while, just enjoying the calm before the day began.

Eventually, we got up and headed out to explore. We drove through stunning landscapes—lush greenery, coastal views, quiet villages. Every turn offered something beautiful, and we stopped often to take pictures, trying to hold on to every moment.

Our room at the next hotel was right on the waterfront, with stunning views all around. That evening, we had dinner at the restaurant downstairs, watching an incredible sunset paint the sky in shades of orange and pink.

Afterward, he said, "Let's go play some pool and have a few drinks." Neither of us really drank much, but I thought, why not? It sounded like fun. I didn't even know how to play pool, but we gave it a go anyway.

The game was more laughter than skill, cue lots of missed shots and playful teasing. We clumsily took our drinks back upstairs, feeling light and carefree. Before we even finished our first round, the alcohol caught up with us, and we were both totally wasted, falling asleep in each other's arms, the day's excitement finally catching up.

When we woke up, we both burst out laughing. The bottle of premixed drink wasn't even close to empty —guess alcohol just isn't for us. That morning, we made love, and as he looked deep into my eyes, he whispered, "I love you." My voice barely more than a shy breath, I replied, "I love you too, babe."

We stayed only a few days in each place before moving on to the next, like we were on a honeymoon adventure. I kept wondering, why is he so romantic? But I loved every moment of it. At one point, I told him that after this trip, we wouldn't be together, but these days would leave us with so many beautiful memories—how incredible this time we shared truly was.

A song played softly in the background, as if the soundtrack to our fleeting but unforgettable journey. Suddenly, a song came on the car radio—the lyrics hit me hard: "You don't love me." I turned to him and quietly repeated the words. He frowned, annoyed. "How can you say that?" he asked, almost defensively. Was this real? Had he just confirmed that he had feelings? Why couldn't I just accept that? Maybe it was because of how he'd treated me in the past.

They say you shouldn't dwell on the past, but what if your past is your future? What happens then? I couldn't forget everything that had happened since we first met. Could I? Would I ever be able to forgive and move forward, knowing he might marry someone else? And if that happened, what or who would I be to him then?

He wants me to be his friend forever—he said that in his email. What am I supposed to do with that? Hold a candle and stand in his room while he makes love to his so-called future wife? I fought to control the animosity building inside me—resentment toward a woman who doesn't even exist yet. And then a thought struck me: what if that woman were me?

He has always been so unpredictable, so maybe this was him assessing me, testing the waters for something long-term. But how do I trust someone who keeps pulling me in and pushing me away? I'm caught between hope and heartbreak, unsure whether I'm preparing for a future together or bracing for a final goodbye.

We climbed up the mountains, and when we reached the top, we stood there quietly, soaking in the breathtaking beauty—the vast ocean stretching out before us, endless and shimmering.

He wrapped his arms around me from behind, pulling me close, his lips gently kissing my neck now and then. The world felt still, as if time had slowed just for us. After a while, he broke the silence. "Let's go take some pictures."

He was always the adventurous one—climbing on rocks and ledges while I captured the moments. There was a huge rock ahead where everyone was snapping photos, so he waited patiently for his turn. Then, with a grin, he climbed up and settled himself on top, ready for the perfect shot.

Suddenly, I had a flashback—so vivid and real that I couldn't explain it. I started screaming, "Alex, no! No! Come back here!" He freaked out seeing me like that, tears streaming down my face. He hurried back, his voice sharp with concern, "What's wrong with you? Why are you acting like this?"

I didn't want to say what had happened. It was like a vision with my eyes wide open, something I couldn't quite put into words. But he kept pressing me for an explanation. By then, we were sitting on the side of the trail, my tears still falling uncontrollably.

This time, I found the courage to speak. I remembered the image clearly—us, but broken, distant, lost. It wasn't just a memory or a dream; it was a warning. A glimpse of what could be if things went wrong. I looked into his eyes and whispered, "I saw us… but we weren't okay." I saw him fall from the mountain in a past life regression. He was climbing rocks when he suddenly lost his grip and plummeted down.

Slowly, I gathered myself and began to explain. When we first met, I recognized him instantly and fell in love. But alongside that love came strange dreams—visions of us, of moments that never happened, and worst of all, him dying repeatedly in my sleep.

I told him about visiting a past life regression specialist, someone who hypnotized me and helped unlock memories I didn't know I had. I shared the details of that past life with him: how he had fallen off a cliff and died young, leaving me behind as a young widow. That's why I feared losing him so deeply—because the pain was already rooted somewhere beyond this life.

He just stared at me for a moment, then asked quietly, "How come I don't remember any of this?" I shrugged gently. "Well, not everyone remembers their past lives. I was told my memories got triggered the moment you came back to me in this life." I went on to explain how, the first time he touched my hand, I started crying without knowing why. It was like something deep inside me had been unlocked. I shared with him how my sixth sense was always quite active—how I sometimes sensed things others couldn't.

He nodded slowly, a new understanding dawning in his eyes. "Well, now I kinda get it," he said softly. I even told him about my dreams—the ones where I was calling out to baby Regina. I reminded him that I'd mentioned it before. "Yes," he said quietly, "I remember you telling me that dream." I nodded and added, "I spoke about Regina during the regression, too."

He stared at me, wide-eyed, like he wasn't sure whether to believe me or question my sanity. I could feel his uncertainty, the weight of it, but I kept going—because it was my truth.

I gently reminded him of all the strange, beautiful coincidences we'd talked about over time. "Our dads have the same names," I pointed out. "And look—" I pulled out my phone and scrolled through the pictures—us wearing the same color outfits on so many different days without even planning it. "It's like something keeps syncing us." I showed him the matching birthmarks, told him how sometimes we just knew when the other was thinking about us. "It's not just a feeling, Alex," I whispered. "It's like I've known you for lifetimes." He looked completely shocked, silent, and thoughtful.

I don't think he fully believed me, or maybe he just didn't know how to process everything I'd said. Without saying much, he reached out, gently took my hand, and pulled me to my feet. "Let's walk down now," he said softly. We made our way down the mountain trail, his hand wrapped firmly around mine the whole time. It was quiet between us, but not uncomfortable— more like we were both sitting with the weight of what had been revealed. When we reached the car, he opened the door for me and waited until I got in. Then, looking at me again, he asked, "Are you okay?" I nodded. "Yeah... I'm okay."

He didn't bring it up again. Not a single word about what happened on that mountain. And maybe that was his way of coping. The final days of our trip were soft and golden, like a movie slowly fading into its most beautiful scene. We swam together in the warm, clear waters, floating on our backs as the sky stretched endlessly above us. We ate too much—sharing desserts, stealing bites off each other's plates, feeding each other like kids in love, laughing between every mouthful. The sun wrapped us in a kind of lazy warmth that made time feel like it stood still, as we lay on the sand like content, sun-soaked cats, not a care in the world except maybe which beach to visit next.

We wandered through local markets, buying little handmade trinkets and bracelets we promised we'd wear forever. We shopped like we were rich, without guilt or thought, just joy. I bought things I didn't need simply because they reminded me of him, of us, and this feeling I never wanted to lose.

Everything about those final days felt dreamlike—almost too perfect, like a delicate bubble I didn't want to pop. But I knew, deep down, I would have to wake up soon. His touch sent quivers all through me—gentle electric shocks that lit up every part of me he reached. Maybe it's because I love him, or maybe his touch really is magical. Either way, I found myself smiling all day, my cheeks hurting in the best way. No one has ever made me feel like that— not even close.

I kept trying to convince myself that it wasn't that deep, that I wasn't completely consumed by him, but the truth was—denial had become my coping mechanism. I couldn't say no to him, even when I knew I should. When he was in front of me, I'd try so hard to be composed, to play it cool—but inside, I was a teenager again, blushing, nervous, completely infatuated.

One day, Jess came with me to his place because I needed to pick up some clothes. When she saw us together, she didn't say much at the time—but after, she looked at me in shock. "You two," she said. "You don't even realize how madly in love you look." Her words hit me like a wave. Maybe we didn't realize it, but the world could see it—even when we were trying not to.

Bullshit, I exclaimed—just last week he told me he still had to find someone his parents would approve of. Yet, we kept seeing each other, squeezing time in despite our busy schedules. I cooked for him often, but there were days when he'd surprise me—bringing all the ingredients and making a meal himself. He was an amazing cook; his food tasted like heaven. I'd sit there watching him, and when it was ready, he'd feed me with his hands, gently, lovingly.

But underneath those beautiful moments, the stress of knowing he might leave me to marry someone else started to break me. Some nights I'd lie awake, replaying his words, his touch, his promises—wondering if I was setting myself up for heartbreak. It wasn't just sadness I felt. It was a silent panic that wrapped around me, growing tighter each time I imagined a future without him.

There was a time, after one of our arguments, when he drove an hour just to see me because I hadn't been feeling well for days. He didn't come with grand gestures—just his presence, and gentle hands that gave me a head massage until the tension melted away. In that quiet moment, I felt cared for, seen, and deeply loved.

But beneath the softness, a constant ache lingered—an unspoken fear that he might be talking to other girls, that one day he'd choose one of them, not me. That fear wasn't unfounded. It echoed in the words he threw at me in frustration, words that reminded me of the reality I didn't want to face.

Sometimes, when my emotions overwhelmed me, I would ask him to marry me. Not because I didn't know the answer, but because I wanted to believe, just once, he'd say yes. But he never did. He'd look at me with a mixture of love and resignation and say, "You know I can't. My family won't agree."

It was always that—love shadowed by limits, care confined by culture, and a future we could never fully claim. "They're looking for someone for my marriage, and I can't take that right from them," he told me one day. Those words didn't just hurt—they quietly began to destroy me from the inside. I had always seen him as more than just someone I loved. He was my best friend, my confidant, my person. The one I turned to in my moments of joy and my moments of despair. And yet, there I was, watching him slowly slip away—not out of cruelty, but out of duty. It made the heartbreak even more unbearable, knowing he cared, but still couldn't choose me.

I did everything I could to be the woman of his dreams. I gave him all the love I had, listened when he needed to talk, stayed when things got hard, and loved him even when I felt unseen. I wanted to be unforgettable. I wanted him to remember me with fondness, with warmth. That even if he belonged to someone else someday, my name would carry a softness in his memory.

But the truth was harder to ignore with each passing day. He was preparing his heart for someone else while I was still holding on. And in that unspoken shift, our love, once pure and effortless, began to decay. We fought more. We misunderstood each other. The warmth that once healed me now burned, and the silence between us became louder than any argument.

It hurt in ways I didn't know love could hurt, watching something so beautiful turn into something I no longer recognized, all because. I had developed full-blown anxiety over the thought of losing him. The more time I spent with him, the deeper I fell in love—and the more terrifying the idea of life without him became. I didn't want to let go. I didn't want to imagine a future where he wasn't by my side.

But I knew I had to fight this. I had to rise above the fear and the endless spiral of overthinking. This couldn't be my life—not a life ruled by anxiety and uncertainty. I reminded myself of the woman. I was strong, independent, and focused on building something meaningful for myself. I hadn't come this far to be broken by something I couldn't control.

No one knows what the future holds. And if God had allowed me to walk this path with him thus far, then maybe all I needed now was faith—faith that He knows what's best for me, and that whatever is meant to be, will be. I had to trust that He....I held on to hope. Hope that maybe, just maybe, he would change his mind—and that his family would, too. I told myself that love like ours couldn't just fade into nothing, that it had to mean something. But the thoughts, they came like waves—unpredictable and relentless. I fought them daily, but every now and then, I'd find myself circling back to that same haunting fear: what if he leaves me and marries someone else?

Whenever I brought it up, he'd start to grow distant, annoyed. "If that time comes, we'll think about it then," he'd say, his voice edged with frustration. "Why can't you just enjoy the moments we have? No one knows what tomorrow will bring. Even I don't know what the future holds." I tried to hold onto the present, like he asked. But when you love someone so deeply, it's hard not to fear the future.

Life got busy. Our schedules didn't always align, and sometimes, we wouldn't see each other for weeks. But even then, we stayed connected—we spoke on the phone every day. No matter how hectic things got, hearing his voice brought me comfort. Then one day, I got a call from Alex. He had just gotten off work early and happened to be in the area. I was out with the girls—we were throwing a hen's party for Jess, who was getting married in two months. Laughter echoed around us, drinks were flowing, and the mood was light and full of celebration.

But when Alex said he really wanted to see me, even if just for five minutes, my heart pulled in his direction. I told the girls I'd be back soon. Jess, ever the supportive friend, gave me a look. "I don't want you to miss out on all the fun," she said, half-teasing, half-concerned. "But I get it. Just don't be long."

Outside, Alex was waiting. I asked if he wanted to come in and say hi to Jess and Arisha. He gave me that familiar half-smile and said, "Maybe next time." That was always his way—close, but never fully stepping into my world. I had learned over time that if I said no to meeting up, even once, he'd get annoyed. It didn't matter how small the moment was—if he wanted to see me, he expected me to make it happen. And because I loved him, I often did…because he would say he missed me, and I'd always give in—just five minutes, just a moment, just because he was in the area.

Alex and I drove to a quiet street, the kind where time seemed to slow down. We sat in the car, talking about nothing and everything. I found myself just watching him—his expressions, the way his fingers moved as he spoke. I gently caressed his hand, memorizing the feel of him, as if trying to capture the moment in my skin.

Then, out of nowhere, he looked at me with this rare softness and said, "Why can't I block you anymore? You know you've bloody taken my heart, Aniqua." I grinned, my heart skipping. His words hit a place so deep I was momentarily speechless. He leaned over and kissed me, soft at first, almost questioning. I resisted for a second, unsure, caught in the web of emotion and everything we weren't supposed to be.

But then he moved closer again, and this time, the space between us disappeared. He wrapped his arms gently around my neck, holding me close so I couldn't pull away— not that I really wanted to. I laughed nervously and said, "Stop it, I'm going to get turned on... I've had a few glasses of wine." I didn't entirely mean it, but I wanted him to know I was a little tipsy. He knew I couldn't handle alcohol well.

Alex chuckled, his voice low and teasing. "Then I'll keep kissing you until you do get turned on." I pretended to cry, making a playful little scene— "Ahh, ahh, ahh"—half-laughing as I leaned into the moment. He pulled me even closer and kissed me deeply, and for that brief stretch of time, everything else faded—the doubts, the distance, the future we couldn't name.

He paused, his forehead resting against mine, and asked softly, "Why haven't you been coming to see me?" I sighed, brushing my fingers over his hand. "I've been busy...

work's been full-on, and I've been helping Jess with her wedding stuff. There's just been so much going on." He nodded, but I could see it in his eyes—he missed me more than he let on.

I laughed and said, "Shut up and just kiss me." Why was he asking questions right now, anyway? The mood was tender, and the tension between us was rising. We were cramped in the front seats, awkward and close, and he must've felt it too because he reached over and gently pulled me onto his lap.

Now straddling him, I could feel the heat between us intensify. My hands slipped under his shirt, tracing the smooth lines of his skin, while his hands wandered across my back— soft, slow, familiar.

Every now and then, he'd gently tug my hair, just enough to tilt my head so he could kiss my neck, my collarbone, and lower, his lips exploring the places he knew made me melt.

The car was dark, the windows slightly fogged, the world beyond momentarily forgotten. Then he started tugging at the hem of my top, wanting to take it off. I froze for a second and gently pushed him back.

"Someone could see us," I said, breathless but firm. "I'm shy, and you know that. Plus… Jess is waiting for me."

He paused, looking into my eyes—maybe frustrated, maybe just caught up in the moment—but he respected that line. And just like that, the intensity softened, but the connection between us still lingered, quiet and powerful.

"It's already been an hour," I said, feeling the weight of time slipping by. "Okay, let's go somewhere else," he suggested, a spark in his eyes. I wasn't sure where he was taking me, but I followed, heart pounding. We found ourselves in a quiet park, empty and still under the night sky. When we saw the toilets were open, Alex didn't hesitate—we slipped inside and locked ourselves in a cubicle.

A rush of nervousness hit me. This is a bad idea, I thought. What if the cops come? But Alex just smiled, calm and confident. "We'll deal with it if it happens," he said, and before I could protest, he pressed me against the wall.

Slowly, he pulled my top over my head and hung it carefully behind the door. Then, with a gentle but urgent motion, he pushed my skirt up and lifted me effortlessly. My head fell back, eyes closing as waves of pleasure coursed through me. I was caught between resistance and surrender, losing control but loving every moment of it.

My back was pressed firmly against the cold wall as he held me in place, my legs wrapped tightly around his hips. He moved rhythmically, rocking me gently but with intensity, his lips trailing down my neck and collarbone. With my face higher than his, he kissed every inch he could reach, leaving behind warm traces—his mark on my skin. I felt the sharp pull as he sucked harder, knowing full well I'd have hickeys to remember this moment by. I looked him straight in the eyes, my voice low and breathless. "I'm done."

He always waited for me—he never let go until I did. But now, it was like something wild took over. He pushed even harder, deeper, like he needed to pour every bit of himself into me before it was over. God, I thought, this man was an animal—but he was my animal. When it was finally done, he gently lowered me to the ground. We were both breathless. He leaned in and pressed a soft kiss to my forehead—tender, contrasting everything that had just happened.

We snuck out quietly into the night, trying not to laugh. "You were loud," he whispered with a grin. I swatted his arm and rolled my eyes, trying to fix my hair. My heart was still racing as I made my way back to the party. Almost two hours had passed. Jess opened the door, eyes wide. "Well… that wasn't five minutes," she said, raising a brow. Jess opened the door and took one look at me—my flushed cheeks, the slight mess of my hair, the guilt written all over my face. She smirked and crossed her arms, leaning against the frame. "You guys have been very busy," she teased, eyes twinkling. "Hope you had fun." I couldn't help but laugh, a little embarrassed, but grateful she was so easygoing. "I'll be back in a sec," I said, slipping past her and heading straight for a quick shower to freshen up.

By the time I rejoined the girls, the music was louder, the laughter even more contagious. We played all kinds of silly games—truth or dare, bridal bingo, those cheeky ones only best friends can get away with. The drinks kept flowing, and the table was piled with snacks and sweets. There was a kind of magic in the air that night—joy, friendship, the quiet understanding that this was a once-in-a-lifetime celebration. Jess was glowing with happiness, and I knew deep down she'd remember this night forever. Honestly, we all would.

CHAPTER SIX

—◆—◆—◆—

People say good things come in pairs

He was what fairy tales are made of. With him, I felt truly special—like the heroine of my own story. I had always been a romantic at heart, dreaming of a love that felt magical, and he was the one who brought that dream to life. Like a girl who couldn't ask for anything more, I was completely captivated. I was hooked on his charms—his captivating beauty, the way he loved me, the warmth of his hugs that made everything else fade away.

Life was treating me amazingly. When he was near, wrapped in his love, none of the world's troubles seemed to matter. I felt invincible, like together, we could overcome anything. Want to build on this feeling with a moment of vulnerability or a shift in the story? Every time I was about to see him, after getting dressed, I'd run back to the mirror at least ten more times—just to make sure I looked okay. But Alex never once made me feel self-conscious. He never said I was fat, even when I gained weight. He never pressured me to look a certain way or to dress up just for him. He simply accepted me exactly as I was. He never asked me to be more beautiful, never pushed me to wear makeup or change anything about myself. His love felt effortless, unconditional.

It was the day of a special religious festival I always observed, and I was feeling particularly alone. My grandparents, who were my closest family, were so far away, and the silence around me was heavy. Then Alex surprised me—he just said, "I'm coming over." That simple promise lifted my spirits. I felt a spark of excitement and warmth, knowing I wouldn't have to face the day by myself. I used to call several times a week, just to catch up and make sure they didn't need anything. Today, he came over—he knew I must be feeling a little lonely. To my surprise, he brought me a beautiful bag as a gift. It had a small key attached, and my name was engraved on it. He just kept finding ways to win my heart over and over again.

I had cooked a lot, as tradition called for it. Jess, Arisha, and a few of their friends were planning to join us later that afternoon. Luckily, Alex knew almost everyone, which made the atmosphere feel warm and familiar right away. I decided to have a barbecue—it felt like the perfect way to bring everyone together. Alex helped me in the kitchen while the others set up tables and laid out the rest of the food. We had a whole setup going—it felt like something out of a summer movie. Alex was in such a good mood, full of energy and laughter, chatting with everyone. But what meant the most to me was how present he was with me. Even with so many beautiful, single girls around, not once did he make me feel overlooked or uneasy. I felt completely secure.

He kept popping back into the kitchen, planting quick kisses on my cheek before dashing outside to handle something. It was sweet, playful—so us. Once the barbecue got going, we started eating while the food was still warm, music drifting through the air. Everyone was laughing, dancing, just enjoying the moment. At one point, someone said, "You two look so in love," and others nodded in agreement. Honestly, it warmed my heart. People said we looked good together—and in that moment, it truly felt like we belonged.

Over the past few weeks, I've been having dreams—vivid ones—about a wedding. My wedding. With Alex. In the dream, we were dressed as bride and groom, hand in hand, standing at the entrance of a grand wedding hall. Everything felt so real—the lights, the music, the feeling of forever. I woke up with a soft smile, the kind that lingers when a dream feels like more than just imagination.

I told Alex about it later. He just listened quietly, barely reacting. All he said was, "Ok." No smile, no teasing remark, just... "Ok." I didn't push. Maybe it caught him off guard. Or maybe he just needed time to process it. I figured the dream might have been triggered by the fact that I was going wedding shopping with Jess and Arisha. It was for someone else's wedding, not mine, but the atmosphere definitely stirred something inside me.

While we were out, Jess spotted a clairvoyant tucked away in the corner of the market. Her eyes lit up with curiosity and excitement—she had to know what her future held. I wasn't entirely sure if it was a good idea, but we went along anyway to support Jess. The clairvoyant led us into a small, dimly lit room filled with the scent of incense and a quiet, almost sacred stillness.

She pulled out a deck of well-worn cards and handed them to Jess. "Shuffle them while thinking about what you want to know," she said gently. Jess did as tell, and once she handed them back, the clairvoyant spread them out on the table like a story waiting to be told.

She didn't just speak about Jess's future—she tapped into her past. Things none of us had ever talked about out loud. Then she said something that made us all freeze for a second: "There are two women who've stood by you through everything. One's an Aries, the other a Leo." She turned to me and asked softly, "Would you like a reading?" I hesitated. A part of me wasn't sure I wanted to hear anything at all. But before I could answer, she smiled knowingly and said, "Let me just show you what comes up. If you feel it resonates, then you can decide whether to continue."

I nodded slowly. She began flipping the cards, one by one, her expression shifting with each reveal. Then she looked at me and said, "There's a man around you. You have strong feelings for him, and he feels the same. He's your destiny. I felt my heart skip. "You're meant to be together," she continued, her voice calm but certain. "And you will have twins— two souls bound to both of you." If what she said was true… does that mean Alex and I are truly meant to be together?

Her words kept echoing in my mind. "There will be people who try to break you two apart." She even mentioned an aunt—his aunt—who would oppose our union. And that wasn't all. She said there would be others, even from my side, who wouldn't be supportive.

We were all stunned. The room felt heavier, like we were holding our breath in the presence of something greater than us. Afterward, I couldn't shake the feeling. It lingered deep in my chest, this strange mix of hope and unease. So I made a decision—I would reach out to a few other psychics. Not to test her, exactly, but to see if there was a pattern… if they saw the same things without me revealing anything.

I gave them nothing but a simple request: "Please tell me what you can see." No names. No dates of birth. Just silence on my end—and a deep desire for clarity. Just a few minutes into the call, she spoke with quiet certainty. "I've connected with your energy," she said. "He has very strong feelings for you. He's your true destiny."

I sat in silence, stunned. What struck me even more was the contrast—when Arisha had her reading earlier, the psychic had told her the man she was seeing was a cheater, just a stepping stone on her journey. It was raw, but honest. And it made what she was saying to me feel even more real—like she wasn't just saying what I wanted to hear.

She continued, "You and Alex will be married, but not without challenges. There will be obstacles before it happens. Right now, he's taking his time—he's reflecting, wanting to be absolutely sure before making any big decisions. But don't doubt his heart. His feelings are real."

Her words settled into me like a soft weight. They didn't promise perfection, but they promised truth. And in that moment, I felt a strange sense of peace. At this point, even Jess hadn't received such a strong and detailed revelation from her readings. It was like the universe-or something beyond us— had a very specific message for me.

The second psychic echoed the first: Alex and I were meant to be. She added that although his family would eventually accept me, it wouldn't be with open arms—at least not right away. "They'll come around," she said, "but not without resistance."

By the time the session ended, I was speechless. My mouth literally hung open. How could she have known so much? After those two experiences, I made it a point to visit a different psychic almost every month. Each time, I asked the same simple question: "Please tell me what you see." And each time, the answer circled back to the same message—that Alex and I were destined, but we'd have to overcome trials before coming together.

There was always this lingering voice in my head—the kind that whispers when you're alone with your thoughts. What if he's adding those girls because he's considering them? What if, when he goes home, he talks to them? As much as I tried to silence it, the fear of losing him clung to me. Not because he gave me any real reason to doubt him was good to me, really good, but because my heart was all in, and that made me vulnerable.

Over the next several months, we went on several dates, each one more special than the last. One evening, we went to a beautiful Asian restaurant. The lighting was soft, the air smelled of jasmine and spice, and we sat across from each other in a quiet corner, sharing dishes and deep conversation.

I noticed something—every time he looked at me, I instinctively looked away. Not because I didn't want to meet his gaze, but because when our eyes locked, it made me feel fluttery and unsteady inside, like I was 16 all over again. His eyes held something that made my guard crumble every time.

For most couples, five years in is when things start to settle—or worse, become routine. But with Alex, it was anything but ordinary. This relationship didn't feel like anything I had experienced before. It was magic—otherworldly, even.

We shared moments that felt like scenes from a movie. Late at night, we'd take slow walks along the beach, the stars scattered above us like glitter on black velvet. He'd stand behind me, wrapping his arms around me tightly as we talked about life, dreams, and the way the world worked.

There was something so grounding in those moments. Then, without warning, he'd gently turn me to face him and kiss me deeply, passionately—as if he needed me to feel every bit of what he couldn't say in words.

Sometimes we'd walk all the way to the ice cream parlor in the middle of the night, laughing like kids, indulging in sweet treats under the moonlight. Those were the moments that stitched themselves into my soul.

We went for coffees and all other activities that we could find, from go-karting to range shooting, movies, and even an arcade. We would play table soccer, and we both were very competitive as well. We both wanted to do better than the other because whoever lost would be the operator, which was our secret word for when we made love; the operator is the one who would lead. I kept having dreams about sitting with his family members, where they were speaking another language, and his mum would turn around and tell the other ladies That's my daughter-in-law.

Then came another dream—this time, I was speaking fluent Greek, every word rolling off my tongue like I had known the language all my life. In another, Alex and I were standing at the altar, getting married. The details were vivid— the music, the flowers, the way he looked at me like I was the only person in the world.

I started to wonder if I was losing my mind. Maybe it was all just my subconscious running wild, maybe I had been thinking about marriage too much. But deep down, it wasn't just about wanting a wedding—it was about him. The feeling that we were meant to be.

And yet, there was no sign from Alex—not even a whisper or subtle hint—that a future together was something he was even considering. What made things worse was when he brought up going back for good. "There's nothing really keeping me here," he said one night. "That's my home. It's where I belong."

He had been in Australia for six years, but part of him still lived in the place he came from. The accent in his English hadn't faded—it clung to his words like a memory of home. And to me, that accent? It was sexy, comforting, and uniquely him. But hearing that he might leave made something inside me ache. I stopped him the moment those words left his mouth. I have nothing here." I looked at him, my voice soft but firm. "I'm here... isn't that anything?"

There was a pause—a silence thick enough to feel. He looked at me with a hint of guilt in his eyes, but also sadness. "But I have everyone there," he said gently. "My family, my friends... all my people. I had a good life back in Greece."

He looked away for a second, as if trying to steady something inside him. And my Aunt Tana... she's not well. She hasn't been the same since her heart attack. I don't think she has long."

CHAPTER SEVEN

—✦—✦—✦—

Marriage on the cards

I felt hurt...deeply. The kind of ache that settles quietly but weighs heavily. I didn't know what I was supposed to do if he actually left. The thought of him going back to Greece and marrying someone else made my stomach turn. And yet, in the middle of all that uncertainty, Alex would still message me. We'd joke around like we always did, and then out of nowhere, he'd drop a comment like, "Yeah, you should wear that on our honeymoon."

It stopped me in my tracks every time. What did he mean by that? Was he imagining a future with me—or just playing with my heart? I couldn't tell anymore, and the back-and-forth was driving me crazy. I was touched by Arisha's boldness—her willingness to fight for something she saw as real between us. But what truly stunned me was Alex's reply. "Don't worry, I don't plan to leave her."

Those words echoed in my heart. Was he just trying to comfort us—or was he leaving subtle clues? Was this his quiet way of saying he saw a future for us? Still, he didn't say much after that. For months, there were no more mentions of honeymoons, no talk of leaving or staying. Just a quiet in-between, where my heart waited for answers that never fully came.

During that time, the dreams returned—more vivid than ever. One night, I dreamed we were in Greece. We were by the sea, sitting at a small table under the sun, sharing a seafood lunch. The view was breathtaking, the air warm, and we were laughing. But when I looked down at our plates, something strange happened—half of the fish were already cooked and served, the other half were still alive, gasping, trying to breathe.

I woke up unsettled. It felt like a message—one foot in, one foot out. Half alive, half not. Just like our relationship. Something about that dream haunted me. It felt like I was being shown that even in paradise, something wasn't quite whole. I called my grandma—she's always had a special way of understanding dreams, almost like a sixth sense passed down through generations. When I told her about the dream—the seafood lunch by the sea, the strange sight of half the fish being alive and the other half already dead—she grew quiet, thoughtful.

Then she said, "Something good is coming your way, but those dead fish? They're a warning. There will be trials before the blessing." Her words lingered with me, heavy yet hopeful. From that night on, I began dreaming more vividly — dreams that etched themselves into my memory with crystal clarity every morning. Each one felt like a puzzle piece to something bigger than me.

In one, I was in Greece—by the coast, the air warm, the light golden. I was surrounded by Alex's family. They were all speaking in their native language, quickly, fluidly, and yet... I understood every word. Even more strange, I was speaking fluent Greek too, like I'd always belonged.

A few nights later, another dream came. We were in a sunlit courtyard. Alex's mother stood with a group of women, their voices hushed. She turned, pointed straight at me, and said something. Though it was in Greek, I understood it perfectly: "That's my daughter-in-law." Her voice was calm, proud, as if I already belonged. I couldn't explain why I kept having these vivid dreams of being in Greece, surrounded by Alex's family, speaking a language I didn't know in real life but spoke fluently in my sleep. Maybe they weren't just dreams. Maybe they were glimpses of a future I didn't yet understand.

I shared everything with my grandma—every detail, every symbol. Then, I told her something I hadn't told her before: that there was someone special I wanted her to meet. Her face lit up. It had been almost a year since I'd visited, and she was overjoyed at the thought of us coming. "Bring him," she said. "I'd love to meet the man who makes you smile like this."

So, I asked Alex if he would come with me to visit my grandparents. He hesitated for a moment, a soft shyness coming over him. "Are you sure?" he asked. "I don't want to mess this up. I'm not good at meeting family." I smiled and held his hand. "More than anything in the world, I want them to meet you."

The very next weekend, we got on a plane to go see my grandparents. My grandpa came to pick us up from the airport. He hugged us as soon as they saw us. I introduced them to Alex.

We drove down to our farms in Western Australia. Alex was a city boy even back in Greece, so he was a little unfamiliar with how he would feel for the next few days. Grandpa told us stories about what had been happening back home all the time, while asking Alex about what his homeland was like on the drive to our farmhouse.

When we arrived at my grandparents' home, we were welcomed with open arms. Grandma was waiting at the door, her face glowing with a smile that melted every worry I'd been carrying. She pulled both of us into the biggest hug, one that made everything feel safe and right.

She busied herself in the kitchen, making us tea the way only she could. The scent of cardamom and love filled the house while Alex and I freshened up. After we changed, we joined my grandparents in the dining area, sitting around the old wooden table I'd grown up beside. There were cakes, warm tea, and laughter in the air.

I hadn't realized how much I'd missed them until I sat there with them again. Their presence grounded me, reminded me of who I was before all the questions, all the waiting. They were my foundation, my roots—and seeing them so accepting of Alex made my heart full.

It was such an amazing bonding time for all of us. The next day, Alex and I woke up early to go to the farm. I got to see my dogs after so long, and they just jumped on me as soon as they saw me. Buddy and Junior were more than just pets— they were family. Loyal, always around, and always watching over us. That afternoon, we made our way down to the horse stables. Momo, our beloved horse, had been part of our lives for over ten years. She was gentle, wise, and full of spirit.

Alex finally said he wanted to ride Momo. I smiled, secretly excited to share this piece of my world with him. I led him to Momo and started saddling her up while he watched, a mixture of excitement and hesitation in his eyes. "I think I'll fall," he said nervously, half-laughing. Without saying a word, I climbed onto Momo and took her for a quick ride, letting the wind rush past us as I circled the paddock. Then, I slowed her down and trotted gently, showing Alex the rhythm, the ease, the trust. When I came back, I jumped down and looked at him with a playful grin. "Your turn," I said, guiding him to the saddle. As he climbed up, I held onto Momo's reins, keeping her calm and steady. "You've got this," I reassured him, my hand resting gently on his knee. "She trusts you. Now you just have to trust yourself."

After a few slow and careful rounds, Alex grew more confident. He straightened his posture, gently nudged Momo forward, and let her pick up the pace. Her glossy black coat shimmered in the sunlight, and her elegant mane danced in the breeze with each graceful stride. The white markings on her legs looked like she was wearing socks—Momo was absolutely majestic.

I stood by the fence, phone in hand, capturing every moment. Alex looked striking, strong, confident, and completely in his element. There was something so natural about the way he rode. I couldn't stop smiling. Grandma quietly joined me at the stable, watching with warm eyes. I turned to her and asked, "What do you think of us?" She didn't answer right away. Instead, she kept her gaze on Alex before finally turning to me with a knowing smile. "I've never seen you so happy," she said softly. "You've always had a beautiful smile, but now… it reaches your eyes. I can see it in the way you look at him—and the way he looks at you. I'm just so pleased you found someone who loves you this much."

Her words wrapped around my heart like a warm embrace. In that moment, everything felt right. That meant everything to me. I just hoped Grandpa felt the same, even if he didn't say much. He had always been reserved, but I could tell he was observing quietly, weighing everything. Maybe his silence wasn't disapproval—just his way of processing.

Back in the city, everything felt a bit louder, a bit faster. But something had shifted. The visit had brought us even closer. I promised myself that the next time, I'd bring the farm to them—invite them to the city, spoil them, show them what they'd helped me build. Because everything I am now... I owe them.

Alex said he would like to own a farmhouse too, and I joked, "Maybe we can build one together." He smiled and said, "Maybe, one day." That little moment gave me hope—hope that maybe we had a future, even if it felt uncertain. I glanced at Alex, who reached over and squeezed my hand. "We'll come back soon," he said, his voice calm and reassuring. "Your grandparents are amazing. I feel like I've known them forever." He'd love to live somewhere peaceful like this— maybe not full-time, but enough to feel grounded. As we drove away from the farm, I looked out the window, trying to hold back the tears. The golden fields, the scent of hay, the echo of laughter from earlier—all of it tugged at my heart.

Alex only had a month left before he would leave Australia to return to Greece. One day, he promised me that when he goes back, he'll try to speak with his family about us—about me. I held onto those words like a lifeline.

There are no words to describe how lucky I felt to have experienced this kind of love. To have had someone like him walk into my life, make me laugh, dream, and feel so deeply cherished. But now, with his departure looming, I couldn't ignore the ache growing in my chest. He was about to leave in a month… and I couldn't help but wonder—was this the end of my love story?

It can't be. Can it? I asked him gently, "Are you sure you know what marriage really means? Are you ready to spend your life with me?" Without hesitation, he said, "Yes." And just like that, my heart soared. I asked him if he truly understood what marriage meant—if he was sure he wanted to spend his life with me—and he simply said, "Yes." I'm going to marry the love of my life.

I still can't believe how lucky I am. The thought of opening the door every day for my husband, Alex Fernandez, fills me with joy. I'll get to fall asleep beside him every night for the rest of my life. Sometimes, I wonder if this is all a dream or if it's really happening. They say true love only comes once, and now, I believe it. I'm so excited and grateful for the chance to spend my life with him.

I went over to see Alex, and he made me a delicious lunch that we enjoyed together. Moments like these feel so intimate and special, like our own little world. I love doing things for him too. I clean his house, sometimes even ask to iron his clothes. Maybe it's my way of showing love, or maybe it's because deep down, I wonder if I'll always have this opportunity.

What if his family doesn't agree with us, even though he's promised he'll try to convince them? I hugged him from behind, watching him cook—so dedicated, so focused, so sexy, so mine… at least while he's still here. I whispered a quiet prayer to the universe, hoping it hears everything my heart hasn't yet said aloud.

I'm trying my best to cherish every moment I get with him while he's still here. No one knows what the future holds, and I'm doing all I can to stay positive—believing in the law of attraction, trusting the universe. But the fear of losing him keeps creeping in, and I know that fear sends out the wrong kind of energy.

It was the week Alex was set to return to Greece, and I could feel the heaviness in the air. I was torn, and he seemed quieter than usual—not his playful, lively self. Wanting to do something special, I took lunch to his work. We sat in my car, eating together, taking silly selfies. He always pulls the funniest faces in our pictures—it's his little way of making me laugh even when things feel hard.

In that quiet moment between laughter and goodbye, I could feel how deeply I'd come to love him—and how much I was dreading the silence he'd leave behind.

That night felt surreal—like time was slowing down just for us. Alex asked me to drop him to the airport, so I picked him up from his place the evening before his flight. I ordered his favorite Thai food, and we savored it slowly, knowing this might be our last dinner together for a while.

We stopped by Jess and Arisha's place so he could say goodbye. The air was heavy with emotion—he wasn't just leaving me; he was leaving behind friends who had grown to love him too. We didn't stay long, just enough for hugs, some quiet words, and misty eyes. His flight was early, and the night was slipping away too fast.

Back home, we sat side by side on the sofa, our hands intertwined, talking like we always did. I had lit candles all around the room—each flickering flame casting warm golden glows that danced across his face. It was magical. A perfect kind of heartbreak, where love and loss stood side by side, wrapped in candlelight. I didn't want the night to end.

That night was filled with emotion—an aching kind of love that wrapped itself around every touch and kiss. He held me so tightly, sensing the storm of feelings I was trying to hide. I didn't want him to see how much this goodbye was breaking me,

Suddenly, he stood up, picked me up in his arms, and carried me to bed. Gentle, intentional, full of care. The way he kissed my forehead, then my cheeks, my nose, and finally my lips—it wasn't just affection, it was a quiet promise that no matter what came next, this moment was ours.

I couldn't let it end there. As he slipped into the sheets, I pulled him closer. My kisses came before words could form. He responded with equal intensity, his hand in my hair, his lips trailing down my neck, every movement slow and deliberate. In that moment, the world faded away. It was just us— holding on for dear life before everything changed.

He hugged me tightly, sensing the emotion I was trying so hard to hide. I didn't want to fall apart in front of him, but he always saw through me. Gently, he picked me up and carried me to the bed like I was the most precious thing in his world. With the soft glow of candlelight flickering around us, the moment felt frozen in time.

As he laid me down, he kissed my forehead, my cheeks, my nose, and then my lips—each kiss holding the weight of a thousand unspoken words. I asked him to lie beside me, and as he slipped under the sheets, I held him close. My fingers brushed along his jawline as I looked into his eyes and said softly, "I love you so much."

He paused, taking in the moment. Then he whispered, "I love you too. I want to have a baby with you." My heart skipped a beat. That confession lit something inside me—a deeper bond, a promise, a glimpse of a future that felt more real than ever before. I was excited about building a family. Suddenly, I could see a beautiful future where we have four kids, a beautiful house in the country, and all our animals.

I kissed him again, slowly, tenderly, with every ounce of love I had. We held each other like the world outside had stopped turning. That night, we weren't just two people in love—we were a story still being written.

That morning felt surreal. Sitting across from him at the airport café, I tried to memorize everything: his eyes, his smile, the way he stirred his coffee. We didn't talk much, just held hands and exchanged soft glances. I didn't want to cry, but my heart was heavy. Time was slipping away too quickly. When it was finally time for him to board, he pulled me into the longest hug and whispered, "I'll come back to you." I nodded, trying to be strong, watching him walk through the gate until I couldn't see him anymore.

I stood there frozen, watching the last glimpse of him disappear into the crowd, his silhouette swallowed by a sea of strangers moving in every direction. My body was still, but inside, everything was unraveling. My heart felt like it had been torn in two—one part walking away with him, the other rooted in place, trying desperately to hold on. I couldn't move. I couldn't breathe properly. It was as though time had slowed down, letting me feel every second of this painful goodbye.

Everything we shared came rushing back in a torrent—his laugh, the way he looked at me like I was the only person in the world, the plans we whispered late at night, and the little promises we made with nothing more than a touch or a glance. I could still feel the warmth of his last hug, the brush of his lips against my forehead, and the way he whispered, "Maybe we'll be married by the end of next year." I clung to those words like they were my lifeline, a spark of hope in the overwhelming fog of sorrow. I didn't know if he truly meant it, or if he said it just to make the goodbye easier—but it didn't matter. I needed something to hold on to.

Even after his flight had taken off, I didn't move. I sat quietly in the waiting area, my fingers tracing invisible patterns on the cold bench, my eyes red and distant. People came and went, announcements echoed above me, but I heard nothing. I was in a world of my own, where everything hurt, and yet everything felt sacred. The ache in my chest was unbearable, but it reminded me that what we had was real. That it mattered.

That it changed me. I didn't cry, not in the dramatic way I expected. Instead, a single tear slid down my cheek, carrying with it the weight of all the unspoken feelings I didn't get to say. I whispered silently, come back to me, hoping the wind would carry it to him. And as I finally stood up to leave, I made a silent promise to myself: I would wait. I would believe. Because love like ours doesn't just end at an airport gate. Love like ours finds its way back.

As I was driving back, he called me just to say sorry if he ever hurt me. I couldn't hold back tears, all I could say was I love you, it seemed like days, 20 hours passed by, I slept with the phone in my hand all night long. As soon as I got any call, my heart felt like it was going to come out of my chest.

Finally, I saw an unrecognizable number, so I picked it up. I heard him say hey in his macho voice, how are you going? My heart dropped as I realized he was no longer even in the same country. That call felt like a lifeline thrown across the miles. Hearing his voice, so familiar yet distant, made the ache inside me both sharper and softer at the same time. It was a bittersweet reminder that even though he was gone, our connection hadn't faded. My heart raced as I clung to every word, grateful for this fragile thread that still tied us together despite the oceans between us.

In a soft, mellow voice, I replied, "Hey babe, I'm good. How was your trip?" We spoke for just five minutes before he said he had to go and promised to call me back later. Just like before he left, we stayed in touch, calling each other several times a day. The first few weeks were the hardest because of the time difference, and he was constantly busy with family visiting him.

I felt myself unraveling, plagued by thoughts that he might be talking to other girls since he wasn't as available. But every time I voiced my fears, he reassured me how much he missed me and that I was the only one in his heart. Those calls, however brief, became my lifeline, keeping me grounded through the long, lonely nights.

I clung to the hope that this was just a chapter in our story, not the end, and that no matter the miles between us, our love remained real and unbreakable. Things were different back in his country families and neighbors would come and go all day long. Friends often stopped by or took him out, and he told me he hadn't spent time with them in so long. He promised that eventually, things would settle down and he'd be able to give me more of his time.

Still, I couldn't help but get anxious whenever I saw Alex online on Facebook or Instagram but not calling me. My mind would race, imagining he was talking to other girls. If he added anyone from Greece, I'd panic, convinced he might want to meet up with them. He hated when I asked questions like that, but I couldn't stop myself

All he kept saying was, "Baba, you have to trust what I say." But living alone and always waiting for his calls, I gradually stopped going out when my friends invited me. I found myself constantly checking his Facebook to see who he had added.

I started weaving stories in my mind about why certain people were on his friend list. The truth is, I rarely accepted requests from anyone except close family and friends, so I couldn't understand why he was accepting so many girls' requests—or even sending them friend or follow requests himself. In my head, I convinced myself he must be talking to them.

All he kept saying was, "Baba, you have to trust what I say." I didn't realize how much living alone and always waiting for his call was affecting me—I stopped going out when my friends invited me. I found myself constantly checking his Facebook to see who he had added.

I started creating stories in my head about why certain people were on his friend list. The truth is, I rarely accepted anyone's friend requests except from family and close friends, so I couldn't understand why he was accepting so many girls' friend requests or sending them requests to follow him. In my mind, I convinced myself he must be talking to them.

He told me he loved me and that I had nothing to worry about. I felt so happy when we spoke, but empty when we weren't talking. I asked him when he planned to talk to Aunt Tana and his mother about us. He said he needed time because he hadn't had the chance to explain everything to them yet.

Still, I couldn't help but worry what if he found someone else? What if his family introduced him to other girls for marriage? After all, coming from Australia, he was in high demand and had received many proposals.

Despite my anxiety and fear about the future, I was deeply grateful that he was finally saying he wanted to marry me and believed he could convince his family. I felt so incredibly blessed that I could have fallen to the ground and thanked God for giving me the chance to spend my life with Alex. He didn't even realize just how much I loved him.

I started questioning him—asking why he had added a random girl and whether he was talking to her. He got upset and snapped, "If I was, would I still be talking to you?" But despite his words, my trust was fading. Two weeks later, I noticed he had added two more girls, and I brought it up again.

As weeks turned into months, the tension grew. This time, he lost his temper—he swore at me and told me to f*** off if I couldn't trust him. That only fed my paranoia. He said,

"If you keep accusing me, I will ...start ... now. I will be messaging other girls."

Then, I saw he had liked one girl's pictures repeatedly. I reached out to her and she confirmed that he had messaged her just 30 minutes earlier. My heart sank. I was shattered. I tried calling him again and again. He didn't answer. I sent messages. I begged him to talk, to forgive me but he didn't respond.

It was just days before Christmas. I went to Jesse's wedding wearing the saddest face, trying to hold myself together. The sight of her walking down the aisle broke me, I cried silently, imagining how close I had been to that moment myself. I could see myself there... walking down the aisle with him.

Alex stopped talking to me. He hadn't spoken to me in eight days. The silence was unbearable. My heart felt like it was breaking all over again each time I picked up my phone, hoping to see his name. I couldn't understand how he could be so distant, so cold, all because I asked a question—out of fear, out of love.

Then came New Year's Eve. December 31st. There was a party, laughter, and fireworks in the air. I pretended to smile, to be part of the celebration, but inside I was hollow. I couldn't even eat. The ache in my chest drowned out everything else. I was grieving what we had, what we were supposed to be.

On New Year's Day, I waited for his call at midnight. I was certain Alex would call to wish me a happy new year. I held my phone tightly as the countdown began, my heart pounding with hope. Ten... nine... eight... I could barely hear the cheers around me. I was lost in my own world, completely focused on one thing, his name lighting up my screen.

But nothing happened. NO CALLS NO MESSAGES

As everyone began hugging, laughing, and exchanging New Year wishes, I stood still—staring at my phone.

No message. No missed call. No "Happy New Year, babe." I dialed his number, desperate. But the call didn't go through. That's when I knew—I was blocked.

My knees gave out. I collapsed to the ground, surrounded by people but completely alone. I didn't know what happened to me; the tears, the panic, the pain—it all came crashing in like a wave I couldn't stop. I had an anxiety attack right there, in front of my friends. The hope I had clung to vanished in an instant.

After about five minutes, my eyes opened and I realized I was surrounded by everyone. Their faces were filled with concern, but I couldn't help it. I broke down again. I was shaking so much I could barely speak. The pain was just too overwhelming. Eventually, as the wave of emotion started to settle, I managed to explain what had happened. My friends comforted me, telling me I would be okay. That there were plenty of fish in the sea. That I deserved better.

I nodded and forced a small smile, whispering, "Sorry...I didn't mean to make a scene." But inside, I was still shattered. I decided to leave the city and go back to my hometown for the rest of the New Year's celebrations. My mum was also visiting my grandparents, so it felt like the right time to be with family. The moment I arrived, I felt a bit of peace. Familiar smells, comforting voices, the warmth of home—it helped soothe the ache, even if just a little.

Everyone noticed I wasn't myself and was clearly worried. They kept asking if I was okay, and I just kept saying I was tired. I didn't have the energy to tell the full story. I looked pale, drained from crying every day. My eyes were heavy, and my smile was forced. When anyone asked, I just lied and said I was fine—probably just overworked. No one needed to know the storm I was carrying inside.

Wanting to escape, even if just for a moment, I booked a short holiday to Queenstown, New Zealand. When I told Arisha about it, she immediately said she would come along. I felt a quiet sense of comfort knowing I wouldn't be alone.

Two days later, we were on a flight together. As the plane soared over New Zealand, I looked out the window and saw stunning mountain ranges and shimmering lakes below. There was something so pure and untouched about the landscape—it felt like nature itself was inviting me to breathe again.

In that moment, I whispered to myself, this is going to be healing. When we landed, our excitement returned. We laughed, took photos, and soaked in the beauty around us as we made our way to the hotel. For the first time in a long time, I felt something stir inside me, hope.

Queenstown was even more beautiful than we had imagined. The fresh mountain air, the crystal-clear lake, and the towering ranges surrounding the town felt like something out of a dream.

After settling into our hotel and putting our things away, we made our way down to the lake. The view took our breath away. The way the sun kissed the mountains, casting golden reflections onto the water, made us all pause in quiet admiration.

After settling into our hotel and putting our things away, we made our way down to the lake. The view took our breath away. The way the sun kissed the mountains, casting golden reflections onto the water, made us all pause in quiet admiration.

We started playing around, skipping stones across the surface of the lake and laughing like we hadn't laughed in weeks. In a sweet, sentimental moment, we each gathered small stones and wrote the names of our special people along the lakeside. I gently placed the stones that spelled "Alex" next to a heart made of pebbles. We found a few larger stones and arranged them to say Love You, Life. It felt symbolic—like we were slowly making peace with our pain and reconnecting with joy.

Tired from the day, we grabbed a cozy dinner at a small local restaurant before heading back to the hotel. As I lay in bed that night, the silence from Alex still lingered in my heart but for the first time in a while, it wasn't all-consuming. The mountains had whispered something to me: healing begins where the heart finds peace.

The next day was packed with adventure. We started with the Flying Fox zipping between towering trees on a long cable, suspended high above the forest floor. The wind rushed through our hair and we screamed with laughter, completely in the moment. After that, the gondola ride down the mountain offered a peaceful contrast, revealing sweeping views of Queenstown in all its glory.

Later, we drove out to Glen Orchy, a charming little town just over an hour away. The journey itself was something out of a postcard, with winding roads hugging the lake and snow-capped peaks looming in the distance. When we arrived, we wandered through the lush parks near the water, soaking in the serenity. We took dozens of photos, trying to capture the magic around us but no camera could truly do it justice.

We found a quiet spot by the lake and sat there for what felt like hours, talking about life. The conversation was deep, raw, and honest. We spoke about our pasts, our dreams, and our purpose. There was something so grounding about being in nature with people who truly understood your soul. We weren't just friends; we were kindred spirits. Awakened, reflective, and learning to let go.

Before the sun dipped below the mountains, we made plans to visit Milford Sound the next day—one of the most iconic and spiritual places in New Zealand. Something about it felt like a calling. Maybe it would bring the kind of closure or clarity we were each quietly hoping for….the mist from the waterfall touched our faces as the boat glided closer. I closed my eyes for a moment, breathing in the pure, crisp air—it felt like healing. Like the earth was washing away all the pain I'd carried with me.

We all stood at the edge of the boat, completely mesmerized. Water cascaded down the cliffs like silk ribbons, and the sound of it hitting the water below was both powerful and soothing. I caught myself smiling, truly smiling, for the first time in what felt like weeks. It was as if nature itself was whispering, "You're going to be okay." I looked over at the Arisha and saw the same look in her eyes—peace, awe, and a sense of something bigger than all of us. We didn't need to say much.

Sometimes beauty speaks louder than words. As I browsed through the photos we had taken over the last few days, a message popped up on my screen. It was from Alex: "Talk to me, please." I stared at it for a moment, unsure how to feel. After everything, here he was again. I replied, "Not enough reception. I'll call later."

Almost instantly, he messaged back: "Where are you?" I paused, then typed: "Milford Sound, New Zealand." A moment later, another message came through: "I miss you." I didn't know what to say. A part of me wanted to believe he meant it, but another part remembered the pain. I looked up at the mountains surrounding me, the waterfalls cascading down their sides, and the peacefulness of the moment.

I slipped my phone into my pocket, took a deep breath, and whispered to myself, "This is my time now. You?" he asked. Oh …. He messaged me, surprised. "Who did you go with?" I replied to my girls.

As I stared out the window, thinking of all that I had been through, I knew I didn't want to go through this again and again. I didn't want him to keep hurting me like this but he thought I was the one hurting him.

When we got back, we had dinner and went for a walk through the town, and some people were doing some street performances. I stopped and looked at all these people doing a performance as we interacted with them. What a fun day, I thought. I really needed this.

We planned our next day as we lay in our beds. We decided we were going to Wanaka and Te Anau and Lake Hawea, we were going to stay in Wanaka for a few nights. We drove through so many beautiful places and took the opportunity to take as many photos as we could. Lake Hawea had to be one of the most beautiful lakes in the world. Deep blueish green water, surrounded by mountains. Some mountain ranges still had snow on top of them.

I felt incredibly close to the as friends. We were having the best time, music blasting in the car as we sang our hearts out. The sky still held light even at 9 p.m., making everything feel endless. We decided to explore a hidden creek with the most stunning light blue water. Driving down a narrow dirt road, we eventually climbed our way down to the creek, where the water flowed gently through large boulders.

Tiny, beautiful fish darted beneath the surface as we playfully tried to catch them. At one point, Jess slipped and landed right in the water, and Arisha and I couldn't stop laughing. I reached out my hand to help her back up onto the rocks, all of us giggling like kids again.

The next day, we made our way back to Queenstown. Arisha had to head home to Sydney soon, and though I was sad to see them go, my heart was full from the memories we had made. On our way back, we made a spontaneous decision to climb Mount Cardrona. We parked the car and hiked all the way to the top, breathless but exhilarated. At the summit, there was a rocky ledge we called "Pride Rock," where we took turns snapping photos of each other, laughing and posing like we were on top of the world.

Then, in a burst of wild energy, we each took turns shouting "I .... LOVE.... YOU Alllleeexxxx— to whoever our hearts were holding — letting our voices echo across the vast mountain range. It was powerful and freeing, a reminder of how small we are in this enormous world, and how big our feelings can still be. After spending hours soaking in the views and the moment, we finally made our way down. It was truly an unforgettable journey, one of those magical days that etches itself into your memory forever.

It had been a big day, so we just wanted to kick back, relax, and laugh about all the new memories we'd made. But in the middle of the night, I suddenly remembered one last thing I wanted to show Arisha. We all got up, piled into the car, and I drove us up another mountain, one I knew would give us the perfect view of the stars. The sky was crystal clear, no city lights in sight, just endless darkness above us filled with shimmering stars and the soft glow of the galaxy.

We stood there in silence for a moment, just taking it all in. It felt like time had stopped. Then, in a moment of chaos, I realized I had dropped the car keys… and in the pitch-black, we couldn't see a thing to find them. We laughed as we tried to put our phone lights on and look for it. Eventually, we found it, but we were scared we would freeze to death on the mountain top under the stars.

The next day, I dropped Arisha at the airport and decided I was going to go see the Glaciers. I drove for 6 hours. I didn't put in petrol at the station. I kept waiting for a service station, and there was none. I had missed the last one. I made it to the nearest motel, and thank god they gave me food. The next day, I was scared to drive any further as the petrol was empty, but the lady at the motel told me that it wasn't far from where I was. I was so glad I made it to the service station.

After getting fueled up, I drove to the glaciers, which were about 20 minutes away. I walked up the mountain with a backpack. As I got to the top, I could see these massive light blue crystallized ice that were everywhere. It was a sight to remember. I took pictures and took mental pictures of it all. A few more days passed, and I got a message from

Alex said he needed to talk to me. I was mad and said I didn't think that we should. he tried to apologize for all that happened, but apparently it was all my fault for blaming him. We started to talk daily, but I was finding it hard to forgive him for the pain he had caused me.

It took a few days for me to forgive him. He told me that I needed to talk to his mother, and he was serious about our relationship. He called and handed the phone. She said yes, I want to talk to you. I have spoken with Alex. I have decided that I want you to be our daughter-in-law.

I almost dropped dead. I started crying, thanking her and God at the same time. She gently said, "Don't cry, my child. This is happy news." "I know you love my son, and you will keep him happy. What else can a mother ask for? Welcome to the family." Yes, I still loved him, but I was so mad for him not to understand my anxiety of being away from him. I had never experienced a long-distance relationship. He definitely has anger issues, for him to go and message another girl and block me.

I knew I would eventually forgive him. I was lost for words. I told his mum this was a blessing, a dream come true.

I thanked her again, and she told me, "I am now also your mother, so if you ever need anything, just call me and talk."

I was truly over the moon. After that, I messaged Alex to ask if he knew what his mum wanted. He said he did. I asked, "Are you happy with her decision?" He replied, "Yes, I am."

Such a happy day—proof that dreams really do come true.

Over the next few days, she invited me to Greece so we could all meet up and discuss the engagement and wedding plans.

The next three weeks flew by, and soon I found myself on a plane to Peloponnese, Greece.

When I stepped off the plane and walked out of

the airport, nerves hit me hard. I wasn't sure if he would be there to greet me or not.

Anyways, I waited for a few minutes, looking both ways, when I saw him walk towards me with a bunch of flowers. I ran and hugged him, and he just picked me up. Everyone started staring at us.

CHAPTER EIGHT

—◆—◆—◆—

Greece, here I come

The plane landed in Athens. As I got closer, doubt crept in—I wasn't sure if I really wanted to do this. The next part was a long three-hour drive. He held my hand tightly, reassuring me softly, "You don't have anything to worry about. We're here." I looked around, my eyes widening as I took in the surroundings—it looked more like a palace than anything else.

"Are we staying at a hotel?" I asked, still stunned. He looked at me with the kindest eyes and apologized. "I'm sorry I didn't tell you earlier, but I come from a well-known family here. I don't like bragging, and I don't want anyone to like me for my money." I was convinced I must be at Buckingham Palace or something.

A man, dressed sharply, ran up and opened the door for us. Soon, a flood of people began emerging from the building. Kids held little bowls, and the women were all dressed elegantly. Then the men started appearing.

I just smiled, overwhelmed, as I heard whispers and murmurs all around. I thought to myself, "Oh my God, oh my God... Alex." They came closer, and the kids threw flowers into the air. The petals floated gently down onto me, and I just smiled, feeling overwhelmed but happy.

Then I spotted a familiar face—it was his mum. I stepped forward and gave her a hug. She warmly said, "Welcome to the family." I was soon surrounded by over fifty people who guided me inside the house.

In the crowd, I couldn't even see Alex anymore, and the language around me was completely unfamiliar. I felt shy and a little lost, not understanding what everyone was saying, when suddenly a girl came up beside me and whispered softly into my ear.

Don't worry, I am here, I'll be your translator. I smiled and said thank you. She walked into the room and said Everyone, try to speak English. We don't want to be rude. She said her name was Salena and she was Alex's niece. Alex had one sister and two brothers. I looked across this huge room and recognized a few faces that I had seen in his pictures, and the brothers all looked just like him.

I felt like he lied to me, and I just don't fit in. I saw Aunt Tana in a wheelchair coming closer towards me. "Don't worry, I'm here. I'll be your translator," she whispered gently. I smiled and said, "Thank you." She stepped into the room and called out, "Everyone, try to speak English—we don't want to be rude."

She introduced herself as Salena, Alex's niece. Alex had one sister and two brothers. I looked around the huge room and recognized a few faces I had seen in his pictures. The brothers all looked just like him.

For a moment, I felt like he had lied to me—that I just didn't belong here. Then I noticed Aunt Tana, coming closer in a wheelchair. I smiled and stood up. Leaning over, I gave her a gentle kiss. "How are you liking our country so far?" she asked. I returned the smile and said, "It's a lot to take in, but it's such a beautiful country." She was warm and friendly, and we had a pleasant conversation. I began to feel that maybe this wouldn't be as overwhelming as I had first thought.

"Aww, thank you," she said. I replied with a simple, "Sas Efharisto," in Greek—I had learned a few words before coming. I smiled and stood up. Leaning over, I gave her a gentle kiss. "How are you liking our country so far?" she asked. I returned the smile and said, "It's a lot to take in, but it's such a beautiful country."

Aunt Tana looked amazed. "Wow, you know Greek?" "Not really," I laughed, "I just picked up a few words here and there." Salena showed me to my room, murmuring, "This will be your room for the next month." I wanted to know where Alex's room was. She told me it was on the other side of the stairs. "I'll go tell him where your room is so he can come see you," she said. That night, there was a whole party organized.

I took a shower and got dressed to go downstairs when Alex walked in, a cheeky smile on his face. He stammered, "How are you feeling?" I whispered, "I really didn't expect this, but your family is very loving." He came over and hugged me. "Let's go down. Mumma is calling you for some tea." We walked down about halfway when they started clapping. I just looked at Alex. That means they are happy for us as a couple. We all sat at the table, Salena right next to me, and on the left, Alex.

Everyone was talking and laughing while Salena kept explaining what was happening. Most of them spoke English, except the older members of their family. I asked who lives here. There were about 20 people who were there, all of whom used to live in the same house.

Everything was fresh, green, and beautiful. I saw that there was a whole entertainment area where it was decorated with lights, etc., for the party later tonight.

Nervously, I came back to my room to get dressed for the party. Looking through my bag, I couldn't find anything that seemed good enough. When Alex walked in with some Greek dresses and explained he went shopping with his mamma and she decided to buy you these traditional dresses, if you like, you can wear them tonight.

I ran over to him and kissed him on the cheek. I told him I was confused about what to wear. "Thank you, and please tell Mumma I said thank you too." All the dresses were beautiful, but I chose the aqua one for the evening.

Around 6 o'clock, people began arriving. I saw over 200 guests gathered in the yard. Alex took my hand and introduced me to everyone. Nearly every person gave me a hug and a kiss. There was an abundance of food and drinks, and the laughter filled the air—people were having an amazing time.

This was so beautiful. I felt right at home, just a very very big home. I heard someone saying something on the microphone, so I turned around and it was Alex's mamma. She knocked on the glass and asked us to come on stage. We slowly walked through the crowd. I heard her say Alex has chosen himself a wife.

And we are very pleased to introduce her to you all. I stood on stage with Alex and Mumma. It was one of the best nights ever. I have never experienced so much love on the first day I got there. Alex said he was taking me to Santorini the next day with the whole family.

He always lived a simple life, and even here in Greece, he still does, but his family seemed incredibly wealthy. I never cared whether he was rich or poor when I fell in love with him. But maybe this was the real reason he had been holding back; he wasn't sure if his family would accept a farm girl like me.

After a few days, we returned to the Peloponnese. That's when Mumma said we needed to set a wedding date, she wanted Alex and me to get married before I went back to Australia. She gently asked if that's what we truly wanted. Alex and I had a long, heartfelt conversation, and we both agreed—we were ready to tie the knot.

I wasn't allowed to be in the same room with Alex until we were married, which by the way, I was ready for until I got to Greece, but now I am double-minded. I am not sure if I can be part of such an amazing family. All my life, I have spent with only 5 of my favorite people. I didn't care because I was just so happy that I was with them. Alex's sister, Lorisa, was also very sweet; she understood that I was from a different country, and she would explain what everything was and its historical significance.

The very next day, we went to see a place called Fira. Houses clung to the cliffs above an ancient underwater crater that had erupted back in the 1600s. We stood there, overlooking the breathtaking sea, where black, white, and red rocks formed from lava lined the shore. As the sun began to set, it cast a golden glow over the whitewashed houses, making them look even more magical.

This place had been on my bucket list since I was twelve years old. Alex had already fulfilled so many of my dreams, but this moment, standing beside him on the cliffs of Santorini, watching the most beautiful sunset, was the one I'd remember forever. He is not shy in front of his family; he holds my hand and kisses me, too. I am just a lucky girl.

As the sun was going down, we started moving to another area where we could still see the sun going down, but when I got there, I had no idea what was going on. Everyone was surrounding an area, making a circle. Alex looked at me as he smiled.

He pulled on my hand as if to say follow me, and I did. He made me stand right in the middle of a circle lit up with fairy lights and candles. I was confused and looked left and right to see if someone was going to tell me what the hell was going on. I looked at Salena, and she just nodded back. I turned around to look at Alex, and he was on one knee, holding a ring box. My heart fell to the ground, though I knew that we were going to get married. Tears ran down my face as he asked in a soft voice. Will you marry me?? I just nodded my head with my crying face. It slid the ring onto my finger as he got up, he held me in his arms, and everyone started clapping. While Alex held me, I put my hand up to show my ring to everyone as if to say I am engaged. It was the most romantic thing ever.

We went to another level where there was an outdoor restaurant completely decorated with lights. We all sat at tables to eat. Salena and Lorisa came up to me and asked me to show them the ring. I put my hand up in the middle of the table so they can see. It was a beautiful 2-carat diamond ring surrounded by baby diamonds on a white gold band. "Oh wow," they all said in unison.

I felt a little shy. I hadn't given him anything in return. Truthfully, I didn't think I could ever afford something so expensive anyway. Back in Australia, he never showed off or acted like he had money, so I never had any idea he came from such wealth.

He always lived a simple life, and even here in Greece, he still does, but his family seemed incredibly wealthy. I never cared whether he was rich or poor when I fell in love with him. But maybe this was the real reason he had been holding back; he wasn't sure if his family would accept a farm girl like me.

After a few days, we returned to the Peloponnese. That's when Mumma said we needed to set a wedding date she wanted Alex and me to get married before I went back to Australia. Mumma was overjoyed, and so was Aunt Tana, though I couldn't help but doubt her happiness at first. But maybe I was wrong. I reminded myself that I didn't need to worry about what anyone else thought. In the end, it was just the two of us who needed to make the right decision for our future.

I had a six-month visa and no intention of rushing back. I loved being surrounded by so many warm, caring people—it felt like home. The wedding date was set for March 21st, just three months away. I told myself that was enough time to plan and pull off a beautiful wedding... I hoped.

Salena and I became good friends. We went shopping for things for the wedding. Mumma came with us for the dress choice too. I had called my grandparents to come for the wedding, and they were going to join us a week before, which was amazing. I can't believe my grandparents would come this far for my wedding, but I am glad they said yes. Alex is also excited to have them come and for grandpa to walk me down the aisle.

The way I have always felt for Alex started to grow even more. The way he looks at me with love in his eyes. The way he pulls me to the side and kisses me before anyone sees. The way he craves to hold me and touch me. I was having a shower when I heard him say Open the door. When I opened the door, he got into the bathroom, pushed me in, and locked the door. He whispered that he told everyone he was going out for a while, so no one was looking for him. We made love behind two locked doors so no one knows, and we started craving each other's touch. Days turned into weeks and weeks into months. There was a lot to do. We were a week away from the wedding, and things were getting

On the more serious side of the celebrations, we had to honor traditions and cultural customs, both his and mine. I was grateful to have my grandparents there; they helped me with my henna ceremony, bringing a piece of my own heritage into the wedding preparations. One of the dance parties held after the engagement was a way for both families and relatives to celebrate our upcoming wedding.

That night, I found myself trying to escape the spotlight. The attention was overwhelming, and I quietly slipped into a corner with a cup of Coke in hand, but Alex's sisters and nieces wouldn't have it. They kept coming over, encouraging me to join the dancing. Eventually, I gave in, smiled, and stood up to dance.

I started to truly enjoy dancing with his family, laughing and swaying to the rhythm. But my eyes kept searching for Alex. He was dancing with the biggest smile on his face, like the happiest man on earth. My heart pounded every time I caught a glimpse of him in the crowd. Then, suddenly, the DJ stopped the music. "This one is for the beautiful couple," he announced. "Alex and Rima, please clear the dance floor." In an instant, the crowd parted, and I found myself standing opposite Alex, completely exposed under the lights.

That's when it hit me, we had never danced together before. The room fell into a hush, and I could feel all eyes on us. I gasped for air as Alex began walking slowly toward me. Then, the music began to play...It was our song—the love song we had talked about when we first met. Our eyes met as he gently took my hand. My heart was pounding, and suddenly, the room erupted in applause. I felt anxious as he placed his arm around me and pulled me close. I looked up at him with a nervous smile, overwhelmed with emotion. It was almost too much. I couldn't even bring myself to look into his eyes.

Instead, I looked down, letting my head rest gently against his chest as we swayed to the music. The cheers and whistles grew louder, and I could feel the warmth of everyone's joy surrounding us. As the song neared its end, I slowly slipped my fingers from his and shyly began to walk away. He didn't follow; he just stood there, smiling at me, proud and calm, while the room kept clapping. Blushing, I quickly slipped behind Saleena, trying to catch my breath and calm the butterflies in my chest.

I hid for 30 minutes before I was pulled back in stage by the beautiful group of girls when the decided to take my hand and push me towards Alex, I looked at him from the side of my eye and smiled as he ran his hand through my hair when the DJ put on another romantic song, oh no I thought as I looked back and the girls walked off stage Chanting Alex and Rima, Rima and Alex this time I tried hard not to feel shy but we were surrounded by everyone looking on. As I looked towards him, he held my hand and pulled me to spin around, then he pushed me on his bent arm.

I looked up, and the crowd cheered even louder. I stood a little taller, trying to steady myself, when suddenly, he took my hand again and started dancing. Then, without warning, he let go… and before I could react, he lifted me high into the air. My heart skipped a beat. I looked down at him, wide-eyed, and said breathlessly, "Please put me down!" He just smiled, holding me effortlessly in his arms for what felt like the longest, most magical 30 seconds of my life.

Then, slowly, he lowered me to the ground. Did I just die and go to heaven? Because in that moment, it truly felt like I had been lifted by an angel. The next day was our wedding rehearsal, but honestly… it already felt like we were married. I wiped away a tear as I took Granddad's hand. Together, we walked slowly down the aisle…

He gently took my hand from Granddad's, and as our fingers touched, a wave of jitters ran down my spine. I knew then, the moment I had dreamed of was so close. My fairy tale wedding was almost here. Living in Greece, I had almost forgotten the life I had left behind in Australia. It was as if I had always belonged here. The people, the culture, the love, they all felt like home.

Everyone embraced me like family, except for Aunt Tana. She remained a little distant, emotionally guarded. Still, I hoped time would soften her heart. It was the week of our wedding. As tradition required, I had been staying about 30 minutes away at Mike's uncle's house for five days leading up to the big day.

Alex called and messaged me whenever he could. One day, he stopped by quickly to grab a shirt he had left behind…As I went into the room and started looking for it, he followed me into the room. I just looked at him as I smiled and shrugged both my shoulders to show that we were stuck and couldn't get time alone. When he pushed me to the wall and held my hands up when I tried to push him away, he came really close to my face, but didn't kiss me; instead, I couldn't help but kiss him. AAAHHH, my future husband. Those lips, I have missed them so much as my lips moved down and kissed his neck. I hear someone coming in. Suddenly, he pushes me away… I sat down on the bed thinking aaaah !!! Nuts.

Uncle Mike walks in, shrugs, "You two are needed in the lounge, they are discussing some important issues regarding the wedding day and then walks out. I look at Alex as he looks straight back into my eyes, and we both give each other a cheeky smile. All day, we told each other everything we wanted to do on our honeymoon, which was booked in Italy 2 days after the wedding. In my head, I was like, can we already SKIP to the fun part? I was well looked after at his uncle's house.

Families kept coming to visit, and I had my bridesmaids and maid of honor. Guess he arrived all the way from Australia. That's right, my girls, JESS and Arisha, arrived 3 days before the wedding. I wish they could have joined me earlier. The night before the wedding, Alex stopped by briefly, just to check on us and bring over some food. While his family was throwing another lively party, we were having a quiet girls' night. I needed it, just some time to breathe, to laugh, and to let the wedding jitters melt away.

We sat around, cozy on the bed, sharing stories, sipping wine, and bursting into laughter. It was the kind of night that settles nerves and warms the soul. Then he walked in. I turned and saw Alex holding a large platter of food. We all perked up; clearly, he had arrived just in time. Jess sprang up to help him place everything on the bedside table.

With his usual calm presence, he came behind me, gently massaging my shoulders. "Come down with me," he whispered, "I'm heading back now." I jumped out of bed as I walked downstairs with him, as he leaned over and gave me a kiss. I had a complete adrenaline rush as he held my hand to slowly kiss it, I just looked at him, thanking god for this amazing man. As he walked out the gate and was about to sit in the car, another kiss on the forehead as I signed with fulfillment, he said Goodnight, see you tomorrow, my bride. All I could do was hold back tears as I waved goodbye. I just stood there until he left. I could hardly sleep the whole night, and I was sure I would have bags under my eyes on my wedding day.

Waking up early, as I had so many things to get through, the cake got delivered. It was so huge, almost the same size as me. We had about 600 guests coming, so I guess it had to be. Flowers were delivered, and it felt like there were flowers all over the house. I had to pack my bags to go back to Alex's house, hair and makeup, ok, not so much to do, but I think I just felt anxious. We only had a few hours, my four bridesmaids started getting ready, Jess, Arisha, Lorissa, and

Salena. They all looked gorgeous. Next was my turn. I had chosen what I wanted to look like in advance.

My hair was curled and braided into a thick, long style with baby breaths. My dress was a soft tan color with a lot of embroidery work and 2 2-meter train. I had ordered a princess gown, which was changeable to a party dress that night just by removing the bottom half of the dress. The photographers arrived and started taking pictures of everything we did. Then they wanted to get preshots in my gown. But I just wanted to go to the church where our wedding was held. Cars were waiting outside as they took some more photos, and then we got into the car.

We stepped into the limousine and headed toward the church, about thirty minutes away. I sat quietly, staring out the window, lost in thought. Jess looked over and said my name gently, but I couldn't respond I was just trying to hold back the tears. All I could think was, I've waited over five years for this very moment.

The thought of hearing the priest say "Mrs. Fernandez" sent waves of emotion through me. As we neared the church, its beauty came into view— three grand arched doors, four elegant arching pillars, and a majestic dome rising above it all. The limousine pulled into the grounds, and we entered through a side entrance into a stunning room prepared just for us.

Moments later, Granddad walked in. He looked at me with soft eyes and whispered, "Aww," his voice filled with pride and love. He wiped his tears and told me that I was the most beautiful girl and the world and he loved me so much. I got up and hugged him as I thanked him for everything.

Granddad, you know I don't have words to explain how much I love and appreciate you both."

It was time to go, and the music started playing when Granddad gave me his hand. I took one last deep breath as I walked towards the door. As the music was at the right point, I stepped into the room and looked across the room, where Alex stood. I stood still for a moment, catching a glimpse of Alex as he looked at me and smiled, then shyly lowered his gaze to the ground.

With Granddad by my side, I began the slow walk down the aisle. My heart pounded gently with each step. Out of the corner of my eye, I could see warm, smiling faces all around us. Then, Alex's eyes met mine, and in that instant, his smile lit up the entire room. I blushed, unable to hold back my own smile as we locked eyes.

As we reached the end of the aisle, Granddad turned to me with tears in his eyes, leaned in, and kissed my forehead. I looked up at him, offering a smile that said everything: thank you, I love you, and I'll never forget this moment.

CHAPTER NINE

—◆—◆—◆—

Honeymoon

As I reached for my dress to lift it to climb up the stairs to the altar, Alex gave me his hand. I could see the love and admiration in his eyes as they filled with tears. We both turned and looked at the priest as we started the ceremony. Which seemed to be longer than usual as I felt the nerves coming through so I kept looking at Alex as if wondering if he will be the runaway groom but all I saw was a very happy man surrounded by his friends and my beautiful bridesmaids looking so perfect, we both read our vows which made us all very emotional.

With me every night, even if I eat early, which made close friends laugh as they understood the joke because they knew I always eat early, so I don't gain weight. He promised to be there in sickness and in health, richer or poorer. Through recessions and addictions, well, I don't think he was emotional as he told it like a joke as everyone was laughing and finding it funny, but suddenly he stopped being funny and promised to love me and support me even through my darkest hours, and never let go. It was so beautiful and heartwarming. I think he was better anyway.

He kept looking at me and smiling as the marriage celebrant said, "You are now husband and wife". He just grabbed me and picked me up, looking up at me. he whispered You look breathtaking, my wife as he brought me down and kissed me. We had a rehearsal, and this was so not planned, but everyone was like awwww.

We had an amazing night as we danced the night away, of course, everyone was there, but I couldn't help but feel like I had the most handsome man in the world, and how lucky I was to have this man call me his wife. I tried to stop my tears over and over as I had no intention of ruining my makeup.

As I silently admired him from a corner of the room as I stood there with my maid of honor, I saw that he looked straight at me as he started walking towards me, as I heard the dj say This song is for the bride. You are the reason by Calum Scott, Leona Lewis, I'll climb every mountain and swim every ocean just to be with you. He held my hand and another hand on my hip as he led me into the most romantic dance. He pulled me close as he kissed my neck. I just couldn't stop smiling. The man of my dreams in my arms, my prince charming, came in a Rolls-Royce and not a horse, but that's okay.

There was so much food I wish I could have stuffed my face, but I was worried I was going to look like a bubble after. Like I couldn't even have dreamed to have such a beautiful wedding, as you drive into the reception area there is an ocean view the hall was glass windows all through so everyone had a view, the tables had a beautiful high vase centerpiece with white and pink roses surrounded by four candles and as the hall was on a mountain top I totally felt like a princess. We had so many group dances, which were so much fun.

We had our car ready to go at 12 o'clock, and we left the party to go to our hotel before we flew out to Italy the next afternoon. It was a beautiful hotel with elegant stairs all lit up with chandeliers. As we walked into the room, there were flowers and candles all over the room, red rose petals all over our bed as well as the bath. There was a beautiful cake also right next to the bed. The bathroom had rose petals everywhere. What a beautiful sight. We lay in bed as he looked at me with so much love. I smiled as we discussed how beautiful everything was about our amazing fairy-tale wedding.

As he leaned over and kissed my forehead, I smiled, but it wasn't my smile on my face, but my heart that smiled. Happiness poured out of my eyes as tears. I moved closer as we lay there hugging each other. He kissed my neck as I looked up. He pulled me closer and just pressed and held his lips on mine for 10 seconds. I wanted to kiss him back, but he just wouldn't let me move, so I hit him on his shoulder to indicate I wanted him to let me go, as he loosened the grip and looked straight into my eyes. I passionately kissed him as he pulled me close, his fingers gently brushing through my hair as his lips found the curve of my neck. I closed my eyes, a soft sigh escaping as warmth spread through me. His touch was like fire and silk—familiar, yet electrifying. His hands slid down the small of my back, drawing me in as though time itself had paused for us.

It had been so long since we'd had a moment like this—no eyes on us, no interruptions—just the quiet thrill of being together. He lifted my top slowly, reverently, like every inch of me was something sacred. My breath caught as his fingers traced my spine, sending shivers through me. I melted into him, the world fading as the space between us disappeared. I gently pushed him back and climbed on top of him, a playful smile tugging at his lips. I rested my head on his chest, feeling the steady beat of his heart beneath me as we wrapped ourselves in a warm embrace. We lay there for a while, whispering about how magical the night had been, our voices soft and full of love.

His shirt was half unbuttoned, and I began slowly undoing the rest with one hand, trailing soft kisses down his chest as I went. He reached to help, but I gently pushed his hands away—I wanted this moment to be mine, to show him what he made me feel. Every part of me was wrapped in emotion—this wasn't just desire, it was love, deep and overwhelming, for my husband, Mr. Alex Fernandez.

Then, without a word, he slipped out of bed and walked toward the spa bath. I heard the gentle rush of water as it began to fill, the warm steam already curling into the air, inviting us into another beautiful moment together. He lit candles all around the room, their warm glow flickering softly against the walls. The scent of roses filled the air as he gently tore the petals and scattered them into the steaming water. It looked like a scene from a dream—calm, intimate, and full of love.

When he came back into the room, he wore only a towel wrapped around his waist. My breath caught for a moment as he walked toward me. I was lying on the bed, trying my best to look effortlessly alluring— positioned on my side, hair draped to one side, dressed in a white satin nightie that shimmered gently in the candlelight. "Are you going for a bath?" I asked softly, but he didn't answer. Instead, he came closer, leaned down, and scooped me up into his arms without a word. I gasped slightly, thinking for a split second he might drop me—but he didn't. He held me securely, his eyes locked with mine, full of love and quiet intensity.

He walked with me in his arms to the bath while kissing me. I was a bit cold and resistant, but eventually slid into the water with rose petals floating everywhere. He poured us a glass of champagne each and joined me in the spa. He sat there talking and kissing me like we were the only two people in the world. My nightie was completely drenched, and his eyes were traveling as well as his hands all over me as we sipped on the whole bottle of champagne. We decided to get out of the spa, and now we both smell like rose petals.

He got out and gave me a hand to help me out, yeah right, I was wrong, he slammed me into the closed door of the bathroom. As he kissed my whole body, I couldn't move because he held my hands to the door, locking it in place. His hands traveled up my wet nightie. Suddenly, he picked me up and I wrapped my legs around him. Alex whispered I love you into my ear as he bit my earlobe. I replied I love you, baby. It felt like our hearts and souls were entwined into one. I could feel the warmth of his body, and I could feel his lips.

The breeze from the open window brushed against our skin, the sheer curtains dancing softly in the moonlight. We were caught in a moment that felt suspended in time—half kneeling, holding each other close, lost in every kiss and touch. He gently pulled my hair back, his lips tracing a slow path along my neck and ears, while his hand moved with tenderness over my body. My breath hitched as warmth flooded through me. I smiled, knowing exactly how to tease him, and gently turned him onto his back.

I ran my fingers slowly along his spine, feeling the way his body responded to every stroke. His soft laughter and quiet sighs filled the room. I leaned down to kiss the back of his neck, savoring his reactions, letting the love between us speak louder than words ever could.

We weren't just sharing a night—we were writing a memory we'd carry forever. The feelings were way more intense than ever before; he was mine, and I was his. There is no explanation for the energy that we shared. As he entered me, my eyes rolled to the back of my head. Feeling and loving every moment. I climbed on top of him as I rode him to the conclusion. By this time, it was almost 3 am, and we were hungry, so we ordered food before lying on his chest, listening to his heartbeat.

As he watched a bit of TV, I felt so incredibly happy lying naked, reminiscing about our love story and how far we have come together. I just stare out the window where I could see the lit up city and a bridge where there were only a few cars. He turned and kissed my forehead, I love you he whispered, looking up with a smile and reaching up to give him a kiss on his cheeks Good night, babe. I love u, baby.

As I closed my eyes for the night. We were catching a flight around midday to our honeymoon tour around Europe. I thought I'd sleep through the night, but I kept waking up just to look at him sleeping. He looked so beautiful sleeping, like an angel in disguise.

CHARTER TEN

—✦—✦—✦—

Nothing lasts forever

Light coming through the window, hitting his face, I lay there next to him, just watching him slowly waking up. He half opened his eyes and looked at me, raising his eyebrows as if to ask how I was. I propped up and kissed him. I told him there wasn't a lot of time and we had to go soon to the airport. As I turned around to get out of bed, he pulled my hand, calling me back to bed. I gave him a hug. I felt something shift under the sheets, oh oh, I thought to myself, we are going to be late to the airport, still laughing in my head.

He put the sheets over me, and there we went again. Ride to heaven and back, I thought, how can I refuse? Mornings are beautiful when you feel so loved. Maybe the whole is better when there is a great start, I am sure most of you will agree. Rushed to the airport but got there in time. Thank god, it was only a two-and-a-half-hour flight, and we got into a hired car and drove down to our hotel.

We landed in Italy and headed to our hotel. It was already a tiring day. After a nap, we decided to go for dinner. We walked down this softly lit street with brick-paved roads. Streets with small pizza and pasta restaurants with checked red and white table cloths, we chose one as we were both craving pizza. We sat next to a garden table with a candle. Wind was blowing gently as I pulled my red Kashmiri shawl over my shoulder. As I looked at my hubby and gave him a smile, I noticed that he was just looking at me with love and admiration. I quickly grabbed the menu as I felt the butterflies. We had some wine and a very yummy pizza dinner. After dinner, he got up and gave me his hand to get me up We walked down the olden day street with a few trees growing on the sides and

We came across a stone bridge and stood there, quietly staring at the river flowing beneath us. The air was getting chilly, so he wrapped his arms around me, pulling me close. Our conversation flowed effortlessly, like it always did. We never ran out of things to say. He had such a great sense of humor and knew just how to make me laugh. He loved to tease me— especially when I started to get annoyed.

At one point, he caught me glancing at some Italian men nearby and grinned mischievously. "Checking out the Italians, huh?" he teased before taking off running, knowing I'd chase after him. "Alex!" I called, laughing as I gave chase. He looked back over his shoulder with a cheeky smile and said, "I know why you really wanted to come here."

I chased him harder, but...I couldn't catch up as he disappeared behind the buildings. Frustrated, I thought he'd just walked back to the hotel and left me to find my own way. I started walking uphill slowly, feeling a bit annoyed and alone. Suddenly, a face appeared from the side of a building and shouted, "BOO!" I screamed, startled, then turned and chased after him again. "You're such an idiot!" I shouted, half laughing, half annoyed.

He sat down on a bench near a tree, waiting patiently for me to catch up. I plopped down next to him, and he pulled me close, smiling. "You must be warm now from all that running." I snuggled into him, feeling safe and happy despite the chill. You couldn't even catch up. I think you need to start coming to the gym with me. I thought it was a great idea, but I was still annoyed when I said Are you calling me fat.

He gave me a kiss on my cheek, saying he wants to go to Machu Picchu and the Himalayas soon, and wants me to be fit enough to climb mountains, as I looked at him, thinking Are you serious? It was a great idea, but that meant we both needed to get quite fit again. The whole wedding and holidays, I have become quite unhealthy, but I am not starting on our honeymoon.

There is no way I am going on a diet while I am in Europe. We travel through Venice, taking the gondola, so bloody romantic. It was more of everything than I could have ever imagined. We decided to drive through all the beautiful cities in an old-style car just to feel the true traveler's experience. I was dying to go to Tuscany, as that was my dream; the green hills truly took my breath away. We got there early in the morning as the sun started rising from behind those beautiful mountains. I told Alex to stop the car so I could get out and just take it all in. I stood on the side of the road with my head on Alex's shoulder.

As the sun touched the hills and the light spread across the valley, we could see the fog all through the valley, which gave it a warm glow. With houses spread across the valley, each house had its own acreage. Alex nudged me to get in the car, so we drove down and got some brekkie into us. From Tuscany to Rome was a 3-hour drive, and he needed to pee every 30 mins. I actually got irritated and told Alex to stop drinking so much water, but he just laughed at me. We made plenty of pit stops along the way, and by the time we reached Rome, it was already afternoon. Rome was a shock of beauty—I hadn't expected to like it since I'm more of a nature person. But Alex was excited to explore the city, and his enthusiasm was contagious.

We stayed the night in a stunning 18th-century hotel. From the outside, it looked haunted, but inside it was like a palace. Later, as we lay in bed, Alex suddenly jumped in beside me and said, "Let's just stay in, sleeping next to my husband." There couldn't have been a better place to be. We decided to get room service as we just wanted to lie back and watch a movie. We ate like little pigs. After a few glasses of wine, I don't even remember when I knocked out. The very next day bright and early we were at Capitoline with half a millennia of history, we got a guide so we can learn from this beautiful city heading next to palazzo De Senteroni for a panoramic view and after that we went down to the colosseum, it was all a dream come true, we spoke about these things while we were dating that we should definitely go and see these places together.

I still couldn't believe I had the opportunity to travel to Europe with my man, my one and only, and my forever. Our family and friends used to call us, but we didn't talk for long, as we were constantly moving from one place to another. Alex let me do as I pleased. If I wanted to walk around the streets at night, he would accompany me. It was the freedom of being myself while having a supportive partner who is going to be there for me whenever I turn.

We drove down to our next destination, the beautiful Amalfi Coast, checking into the Excelsior Grand Hotel with some of the most beautiful views. We were so excited to go out and start exploring, me being me, always hungry, I needed to go asap because my tummy started hurting. We walked up the stairs out of the hotel, where Alex saw a baby goat on the road bleating, pretty sure it was lost. Alex said I'll put him on the other side of the fence and he ran to pick it up and put him on the other side of the fence.

I stood there waiting for him when suddenly I heard a truck speeding out of nowhere. I screamed at Alex to move, but there was no space for him to get out of the way—the other side of the road was blocked by a brick wall. I ran toward the truck, but it was too late. I screamed so loud that the truck finally stopped about five meters away. I fell to my knees, crying and begging Alex to get up. He lay on the road, lifeless, with so much blood around him. I was in shock, inconsolable......I screamed for help.

People gathered quickly, and a man named Richard came to help. Together, we carefully put Alex in his car and rushed him to the hospital. I was covered in blood. The doctors took over from there... They took him into surgery, and I stood outside for 3 hours praying and shaking. I called his mum and told her the bad news; she was shaken. They got the next available flight so they could be next to him. Doctors came out and said that he is stable, but they can't promise anything.

The next day, all of Alex's family arrived. We all tried so much to console each other, but nothing was working.

Alex had also suffered a cardiac arrest and had gone into a coma. he was in a coma for 2 months, and we all prayed day and night. I kept feeling dizzy, but thought it was because I was always so stressed out. I sat there watching my husband fade away. I tried to talk to him. I was sure his soul could hear my words, I love u, baby, now and forever, you will be back on your feet in no time, all these masks and wires just made me feel helpless. I couldn't help the man I loved to get better; money couldn't make my darling Alex better; even the best doctors couldn't make him get up.

Five days had passed when I saw movement, and suddenly, I was hopeful. His fingers trembled over mine. Omg, he's going to be ok, I told his family with tears running down my face. His mum pulled me and hugged me. I hope so, my darling. He will get better soon. One of the nurses suggested that I should get a blood test, and I did, but found out I was pregnant. I was so happy that a little Alex was growing inside of me. I would tell Alex and hope he could hear me and fight harder to come out of the coma. I would tell him of all the things we would do when the baby arrived and how we were going to be parents.

I couldn't make myself leave him and go; I wanted to see him open his eyes just once. Alex had several broken bones, stitches all over his face, and half his body had turned blue because doctors couldn't stop his internal bleeding I went back into the ICU and as I touched his bandaged hands and fingers, I saw his eyes move around and I called the nurse, she said hopefully he will wake up soon, gently talk to him she advised a few hours past when he suddenly opened his eyes and looked straight at me saying where am I.

I said My darling, you are in the hospital, you had a car accident, he said he didn't remember anything other than a sudden pain. I ran out and told his family he woke up, and everyone was so happy to talk to him again. The nurse told everyone to let him rest. I was the only one allowed to stay with him. He was drifting in and out of consciousness from the heavy medication.

Then suddenly, he opened his eyes and looked straight at me. "I don't think I'll make it," he whispered, struggling to breathe. My heart shattered. I held his hand tightly, fighting back tears. "Baby, I love you. I'm right here," I whispered back, trying to stay strong for him. I quickly called the nurse. She rushed in and began checking his vitals. His temperature was dangerously high, and his blood pressure had dropped too low.

She looked at me with concern and called for the doctors immediately. "Please wait outside," she said gently. I didn't want to leave. My feet felt rooted to the floor. But I had no choice. I stepped out of the room, praying. Through the small glass window, I saw the doctors rushing in. I could hear the urgency in their voices as they tried to revive him.

He was slowly fading away... I couldn't take it, I cried my eyes out as I fell down on my knees and prayed to god not to take him from me. I called everyone back to the hospital. I was going crazy. A couple of doctors came out as I looked at their faces for good news. They told us to sit down. I knew they had been able to save him. He can't just leave me here and go.

The doctor explained that he had another cardiac arrest and that they couldn't save him. Aaaallllllleeeeeeeeeeeeeeeeee exxxxxxxxxxxxxxxxxxxxxxxxxx. I screamed, "Nooooo! You can't leave me like this!" His body went into shock, and chaos broke out around me. Someone grabbed me as I fell to the floor. I couldn't breathe—every breath felt like knives. They rushed me to another room and placed an oxygen mask over my face, but nothing helped. I was shaking uncontrollably, my entire body overwhelmed with grief and panic. "They have to be lying," I kept telling myself. "They can't say this to me. My Alex won't just leave me like this..."

Looking back, I see the strength it took to survive. I was sitting on a weathered bench beneath the shelter of an old tree. I looked out at the quiet expanse before me. There was no one in sight—just rows of beautifully carved headstones and fresh flowers gently swaying in the breeze. The graveyard, for reasons I couldn't always explain, felt more like home than anywhere else. It was peaceful here.

Honest. The world outside moved too fast, but here, everything slowed down enough for me to breathe. Thirteen years had passed since the day my life was shattered—the day I became the widow of Alex Fernandez. It still felt surreal saying those words, even now. So much time had gone by, and yet the pain never fully disappeared. It changed shape. It became quieter, more manageable, but it never left.

Looking back, I see the strength it took to survive. I clawed my way out of the deep, dark pit of depression and anxiety. There were days when getting out of bed felt impossible, when the weight on my chest was so heavy I thought it would crush me. I didn't want to live. The truth is— I tried to end it all more than once. But even in those moments of unbearable grief, something inside me held on. I couldn't bring myself to go through with it. Maybe it was fear. Maybe it was love. Maybe, deep down, I knew Alex wouldn't have wanted that for me.

Family and friends surrounded me with love, always trying their best to be supportive throughout the years. They wanted me to get better—to find the strength to heal. But grief doesn't follow a timeline. It doesn't respond to well-meaning advice or kind words. I was traumatized to the core, paralyzed by the weight of loss. Some days, I simply couldn't move. I would sit in the same spot for hours, staring blankly out the window, watching the world go by without me.

There were days—many of them—where I sat with silent tears, my soul begging for the impossible. All I wanted was to dig Alex out of the grave, just to hold him one more time. Just to tell him how much I loved him. Just to feel his arms around me again, even if only for a moment. It wasn't about denial. It was about desperation—an ache so deep that it made breathing feel like a burden.

This void... it's permanent. A part of me was buried with him. Death didn't just take Alex away—it tore us apart, ripped the fabric of our shared dreams, and left me clinging to memories. No amount of time will ever fill that empty space. I've come to accept that. But acceptance doesn't mean the pain is gone. It just means I've learned to carry it.

Deep down, I knew, I knew he was gone in this lifetime. I knew no amount of crying, praying, or pleading would bring him back. The pain of losing him was unbearable—it didn't just break my heart; it shattered my soul. It felt as though something sacred had been ripped from within me, leaving behind a silence that echoed louder than any scream.

Just when I thought I couldn't endure any more, when I was already crawling through the darkest depths of grief, the universe struck again. I lost the only part of him I had left— our baby. That loss broke me in a way nothing else ever had.

It was more than just a miscarriage; it felt like my last tie to Alex had been severed. The hope I held onto, the dream of holding a piece of him in my arms, of watching a part of him live on through our child—that dream was gone. And with it, any remaining illusion that life would ever feel whole again.

I crumpled under the weight of it all. There were no words, no prayers, no comfort that could reach me in that place. It was just me, the grief, and the unbearable silence of everything I'd lost. Within the same week, I lost both my husband and our child.

Two heartbeats that once gave my life meaning were silenced in the blink of an eye. It was too much, too cruel, too devastating to comprehend. I wasn't just grieving—I was destroyed. Not just broken... I was completely shattered. There's a difference. Broken implies something that can be repaired, something that can be pieced back together with time and care.

But I was beyond that. I was in ruins—emotionally, spiritually, physically. My world had collapsed, and I was buried beneath the rubble of what used to be my dreams, my hopes, my future. Every breath was a reminder of what I had lost. Every heartbeat felt like a betrayal—how could mine continue when theirs had stopped?

I remember looking at myself in the mirror during those days and not recognizing the woman staring back. Her eyes were hollow, her face pale, her soul absent. I felt like a ghost trapped in a body, wandering through a world that no longer felt like home. The pain was not just in my heart—it lived in my bones, in my breath, in every silent second that passed without them. And still, somehow, I survived.

One day, in the quiet of my grief, I picked up a pen and a piece of paper and began to write down all the things Alex and I had dreamed of doing together. Every little plan, every whispered wish, every "one day" became a line on that page. It was longer than I expected, because we were dreamers. We both loved the outdoors. We had always talked about hiking through ancient forests, kayaking in crystal-clear lakes, and chasing sunrises on mountaintops. Our list wasn't just places to go—it was moments we had planned to live.

And for the past ten years, I've been doing just that. I've honored him the only way I knew how—by living the life we imagined. I've traveled the world, stood in places we once marked on maps, and climbed mountains I never believed I could. I've walked through valleys where the air was so still it felt like he was walking beside me. I've taken photos in places we dreamed of, always leaving a part of him there.

You see, Alex was a mountaineer. Before we met, he had already conquered Kilimanjaro in Tanzania. He spoke of it with such awe, like it wasn't just a mountain, but a spiritual journey. He'd also climbed the Matterhorn, his eyes lighting up every time he recalled the rush of standing at the top, the wind whipping around him like a badge of triumph. I used to listen to those stories with admiration, thinking I could never do something like that. But I did. For him. For us.

First stop: Swat Valley.

The mountains stood tall like silent guardians, wrapped in mist, their snow-kissed peaks touching the sky. The air was crisp, and the rivers shimmered under the sun.

My bucket list… I've not only ticked off everything on it, but I've even experienced things I never imagined would be on it.

Alex gave me life again, even though he's no longer here.

It's never been the same without him, and it never will be—but I've kept moving forward. Along the way, I've made beautiful connections and friendships that brought light into my darkest days.

My first trip was through Pakistan.

I couldn't believe how breathtakingly beautiful this country was. The people—warm, welcoming, and honestly the friendliest bunch I've ever met— treated me like family. They wouldn't let me leave home without stuffing me with food until I couldn't move.

One of the places I was determined to visit was Gilgit. But on the way there, I made sure to explore a few gems, covered in snow, surrounded by greenery and running rivers, heaven on earth for sure, felt like I had seen it all, we stayed in a place called Chitral on the foot of the K2 mountain range, we all got up early to start our journey towards the Kailash valley, the roads where it was so small that hardly one car could pass, every time we started to drive a little faster, I would literally hold my breath as there was nothing there to stop us from falling down these mountains, on our way there, we stopped on top, near the edge.

Near a scenic view site, you can stare out into the mountain ranges, fields, and farming lakes and rivers running through, and small waterfalls, which we stopped several times to drink from; they said it was spring.

God has given me a new Start in life, when I thought I couldn't breathe. I look up and see someone walk in through the gates, and a smile appears on my face. He came and sat next to me near Alex's grave, hi Alex, he said, and hey u....

I turn around and give him a kiss. "Hi honey, sorry I lost track of time," I said. It was my boyfriend, Jason, who is truly my rock, my peace, my reason to live again. He gave me my smile back; he is my travel buddy and my partner in crime. Truly wish I had met him earlier, but better late than never, I say. He showed me how to love again. He showed me that true love does exist when I had no hope and wanted to die.

He loved me when I couldn't even love myself. I believe god sent him to me for a reason. To make me see that this isn't the end. He has the kindest soul.

Together, we've traveled across the world, not just to see places but to help people. People in need. People in pain. We've found our purpose in service, especially to those struggling with depression and unable to see a way forward. It's become our mission: to remind them that there is light after darkness.

Even though Alex is no longer here in the physical sense, I feel him with me in every step. He walks beside me in spirit, guiding me through this journey with strength and love. My life now is deeply spiritual.

Through the darkest times, I awakened. I realized what the world is truly about: connection, compassion, and consciousness. I meditate every day. I've learned to ground

125

myself in the present, to listen to the quiet whisper of peace that lives inside all of us.

Alex will always live in my heart. I know he surrounds me, cheering me on, and all he wants is for me to be happy. Having spent years in depression and panic attacks using pills to keep myself sane, to now loving life hasn't been easy. It was taking the first steps that was hard, but I had to for no one but myself.

Choosing a different life and accepting changes. Learning the universe works in mysterious ways and whatever happens is for our better, even when we can't see what the next step is. I travel the world with Jason, stand on top of mountains, and feel the cold air as I see the world in front of me. Put my feet in oceans and sit around fireplaces, meet new people, and I thank god for the many opportunities he has given me.

Learning is self-love. Making goals and focusing on achieving them helps with getting out of depression. Follow your heart, meditate, and best of all, your journey will come with ups and downs.

My life, and my memories of Alex, will never change. Everything I felt, I wrote down in my diary. I wanted the world to know:

Yes, twin flames do exist.

Even if he left too soon, Alex is the reason I believe in love. He is the reason I awakened spiritually. He is the reason I found my true purpose. I still visit his family whenever I can. They continue to welcome me with open arms, treating me like one of their own—even to this day.

Life is never easy. But we can make it beautiful if we choose to. There were years I couldn't see that. I sat inside my house for three long years, paralyzed by panic attacks. I would shake uncontrollably, crying until I could barely breathe. The grief had taken over my body, my mind, and my spirit.

"As you awaken, you will come to understand that the journey to love isn't about finding the one; the journey is about becoming the one.

- Creig Crippen

www.ingramcontent.com/pod-product-compliance
Lightning Source LLC
Chambersburg PA
CBHW060630130626
46555CB00002B/743